How to Paint
A Still Life
In Watercolor
Silver and Cherries

by Debbie Waldorf Johnson

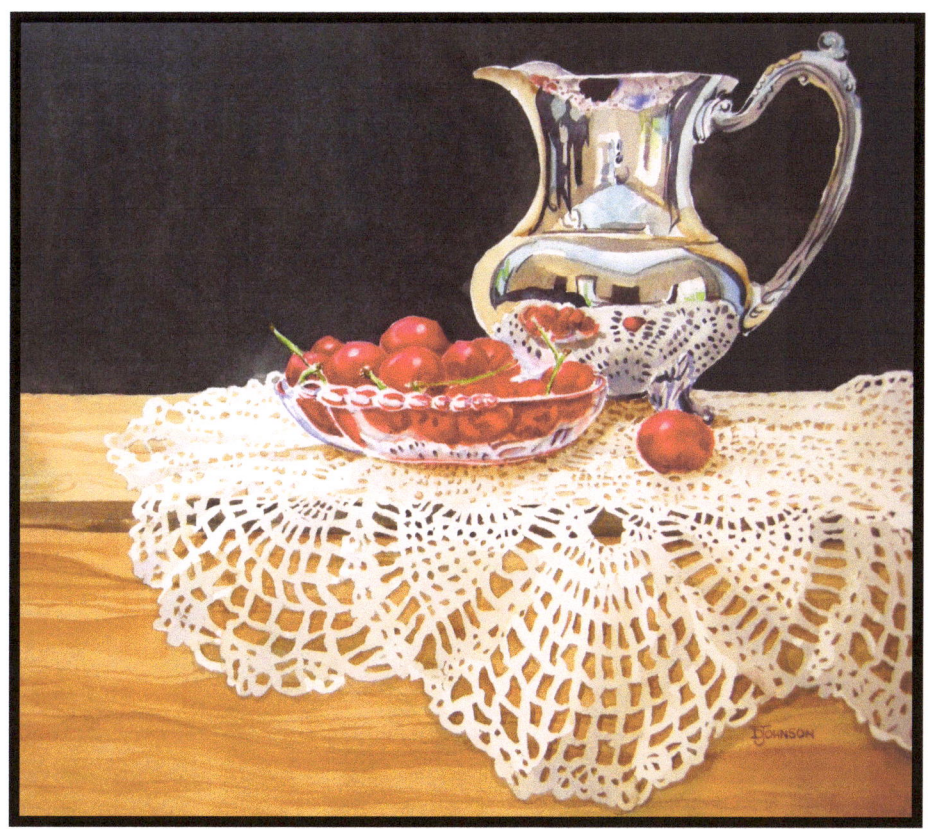

Copyright © 2014 by Debbie Waldorf Johnson

Table of Contents

Review of Basic Painting Skills

Before starting your project, review some of the basic skills required in watercolor painting.

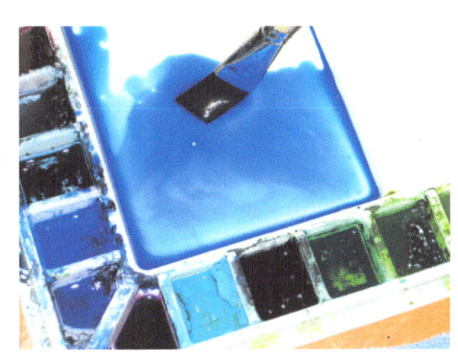

When preparing for a wash (application of paint in a watercolor painting) always begin with a big puddle of wet paint in your palette.

Draw four loose rectangles on a piece of watercolor paper. Each rectangle should be about four by five inches, approximately. Draw these loosely; there is no need to use a ruler! Use these four rectangles to practice the following basic painting skills.

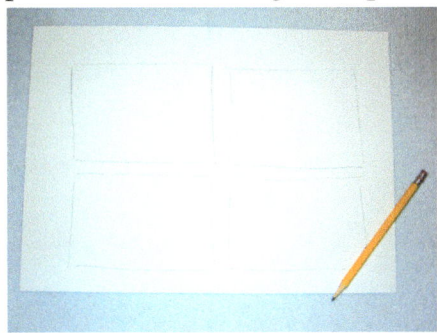

Flat Wash - an even distribution of color in a small or large area. This is the foundational wash for all other washes used in watercolor painting.

Hold your paper in your non-painting hand at a slight angle resting the side of the paper that is closest to your palette on the table and lifting the other edge of the paper about 25-35 degrees above the table. Start at the high end so that your paint will float toward the next stroke. Using a one-inch flat wash brush, draw a wet line of paint across the rectangle from the far edge toward the edge that is

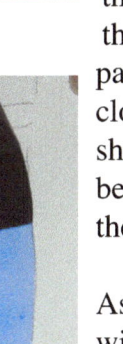

closest to your body.. The paint should be wet enough to leave a bead or puddle of wet paint along the edge of your mark.

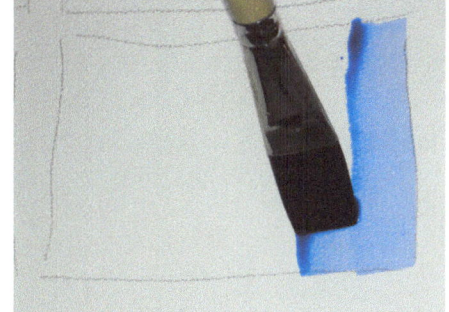

As you pull the next stroke, again with very wet paint, be sure it touches the puddle or bead of paint from the previous stroke. This pulls the wetness into the next stroke. Continue holding the paper at a slight angle to keep the bead at the bottom edge of the stroke so that you can touch it again when making the next stroke.

When you completely fill the rectangle, touch your brush on a paper towel or an old wash cloth, and use the relatively dried brush to

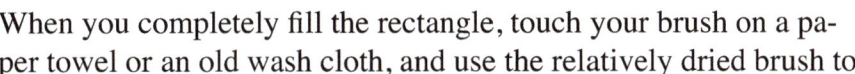

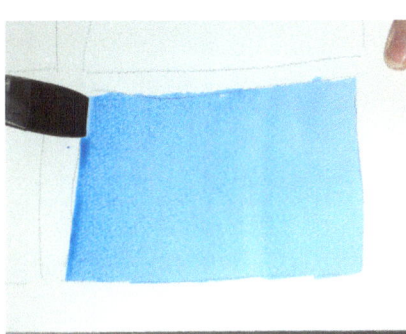

syphon the last bead of paint away from the wash. Now it is safe to lay the paper flat again. Allow the paper to dry or dry with a hair dryer. If using a hair dryer hold it at a distance so that the air does not move the pigment particles that are floating in the wet paint.

The goal of a flat wash is to create a flat, smooth area of even color.

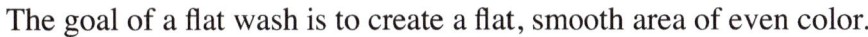

View a video of this technique at:
http://www.youtube.com/watercolorworks

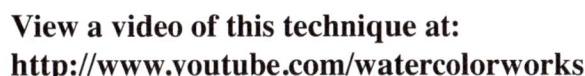

Graded Wash – a wash that starts with a darker value and progresses to a lighter value.
The same principle that is used for a flat wash is also used in creating a graded wash. The difference is that as each stroke is applied, a small amount of water is added to the brush to make the pigment more diluted. This creates a nice value change, which can be used in almost every painting. It is especially great for skies.

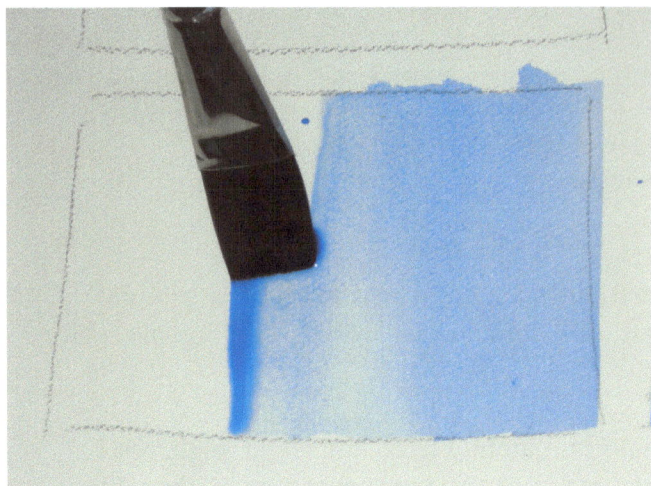 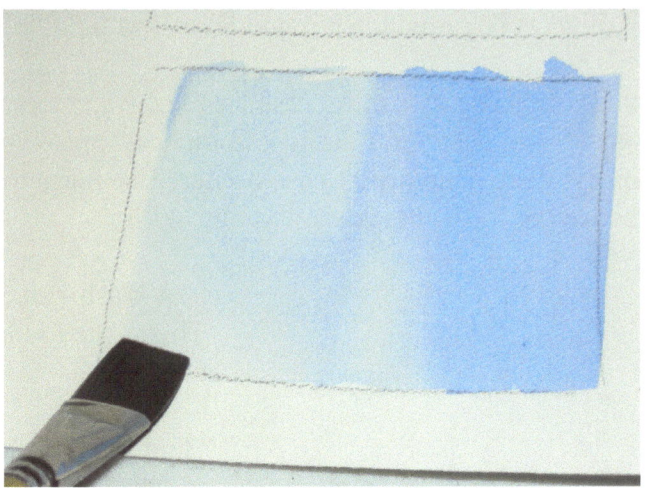

Blended Wash – a wash that contains two or more colors that meet at wet edges to blend together and appear soft.

Again use the same technique to lay down color as you would a flat wash. This time, clean your brush and change pigment part way through. Notice that as the second color touches the bead of the first color, it creates a soft edge. If both colors are very wet and the paper is tipped back and forth, they will physically mix to create a soft blend of new color.

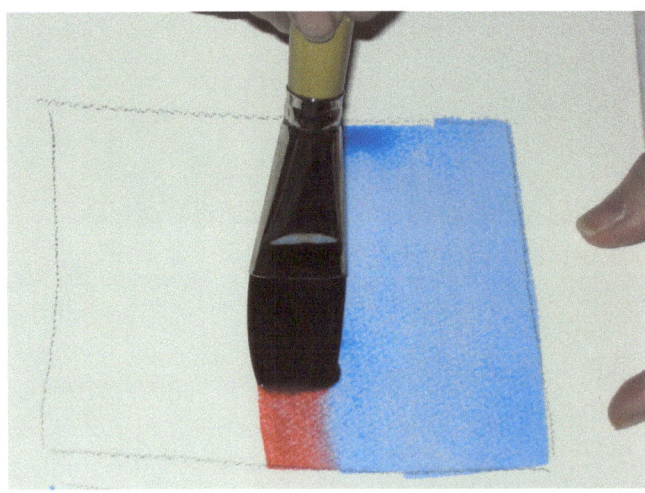 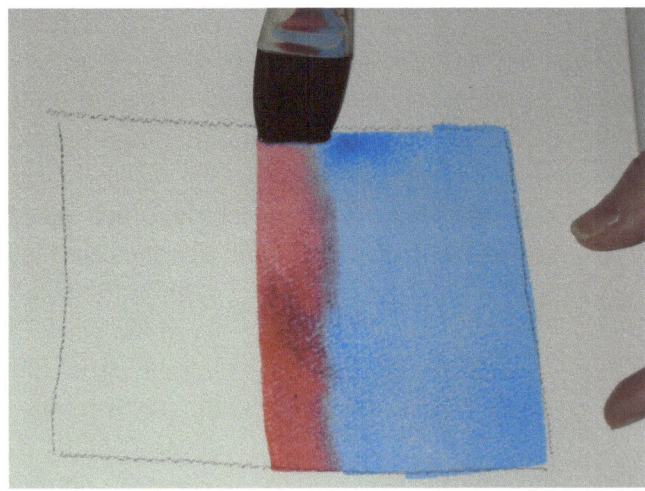

View a video of this technique at:
http://www.youtube.com/watercolorworks

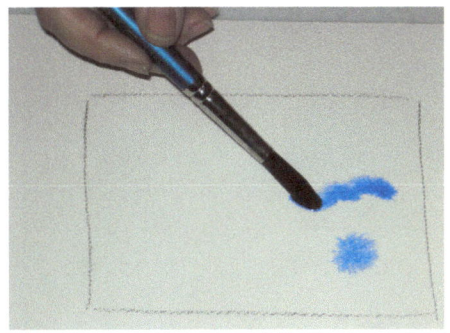 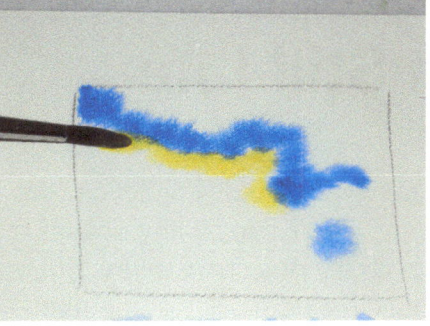 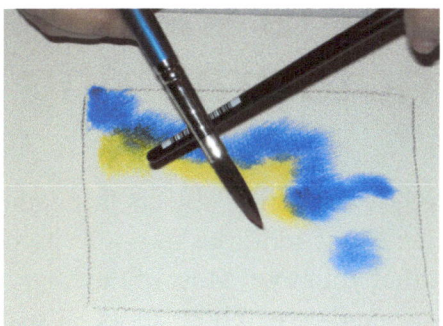

Wet-in-Wet Wash – a varied wash of several colors applied on a wet surface.

Wet-in-wet washes are fun, yet difficult to control. Wet one of your rectangles with plain water or a light color. Completely cover the rectangle. Allow the water to absorb into the paper so there are no standing puddles, but you do want a glossy appearance to the area.

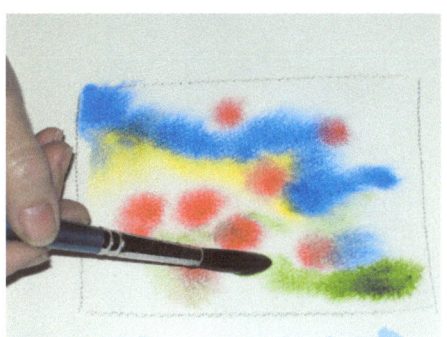

Next, drip or paint strong pigments into the wet areas. Use several colors and experiment. You can also tap a loaded brush onto the handle of another brush to splash pigment into the wet area. Tipping the paper will blend the colors more; leaving the paper flat will help to control the blending.

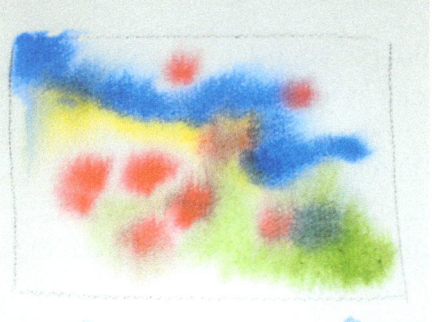

Calligraphic Linework – line work of pigment developed using all edges of a brush at various angles. Practice using all of your brushes and see how many marks you can make with each. Hold the brush straight up and down, hold it at a drastic angle, and push and lift it as you pull pigment across the paper. Try to write your name in cursive with each brush you have. Explore what your brushes can do for you!

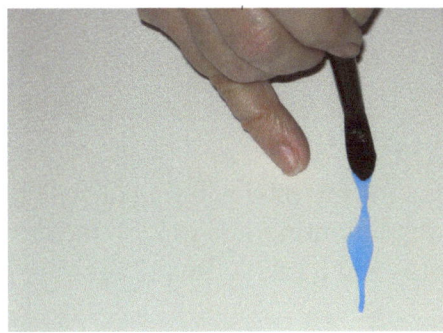 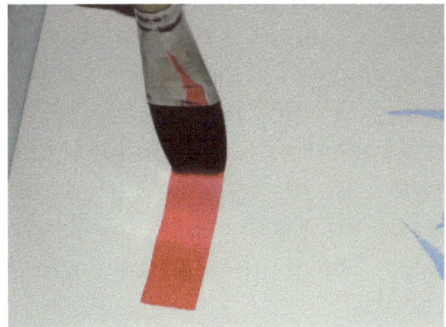 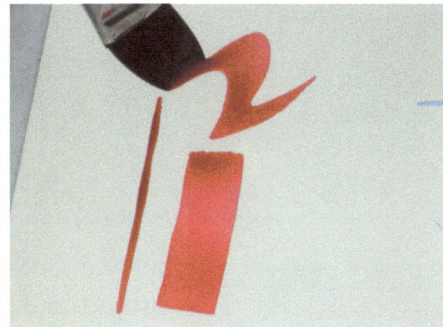

Dry Brush/Scumble – line work of pigment developed using relatively dry paint and a variety of brush strokes. Use less pigment in an almost-dry brush to create sketchy, expressive strokes with a variety of brushes. This is a great technique to develop textures in wood or natural objects.

View a video of this technique at:
http://www.youtube.com/watercolorworks

Setting Up and Photographing a Still Life

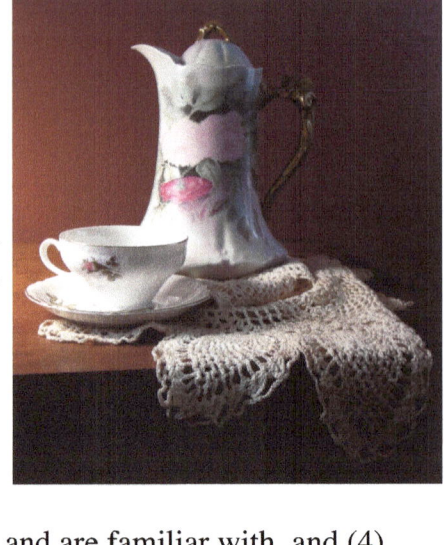

I enjoy collecting objects that excite my eye and that I believe make interesting additions to a still life design. These can be any objects that attract your eye. Most of the time I set up the objects in many different ways and do a "photo shoot." I rearrange the items, adjust the lighting, and mix things up. All the while I use my digital camera to record

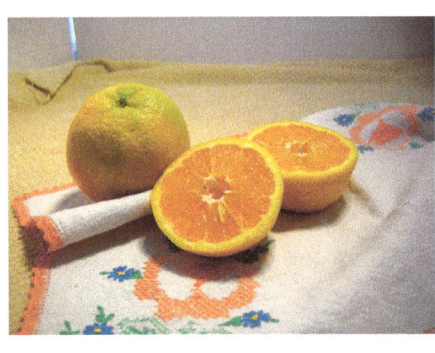

the process. Some rules of thumb: (1) use odd numbers of objects, (2) control the light sources so you can have strong lights and shadows, (3) use objects that you enjoy looking at and are familiar with, and (4) keep it simple.

I like to light most of my still life setups from the upper left. I use cardboard or other objects to block unwanted ambient light sources. I have a small spotlight with a metal reflective top that clamps onto just about anything. It swivels easily so I can control the focal point of the light. I can easily move the light on a setup for a dramatic affect. I also enjoy using fabric, doilies, napkins, and quilts as props along with my objects. They add warmth and interest. It is a good idea to spend a day or two photographing objects to get the right setup, view, and lighting. Once I get started in the painting process, I work from these photos so that I have no time or lighting constraints.

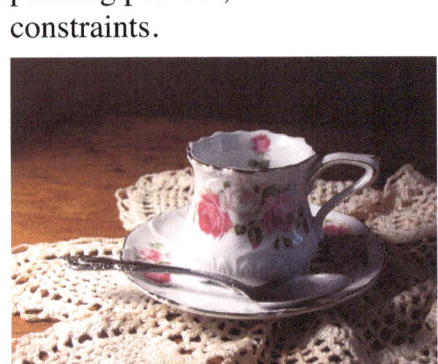

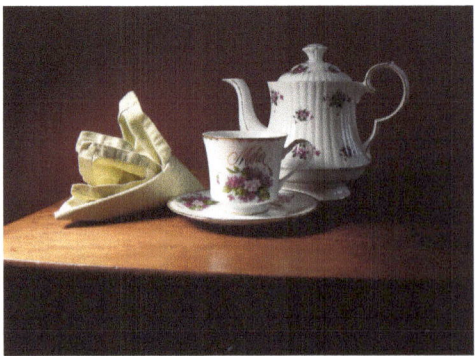

Always use your own photos!!! Collecting and organizing photos from magazines and other sources is fun and provides rich resources for inspiration for your paintings. I enjoy looking at professional photographs as inspiration for setups, but I always use my own objects and photos for my own paintings. Once you take photos that suit your desires for a painting it is time to move on to the next step. I have provided reference photos and a final drawing for the project in this book.

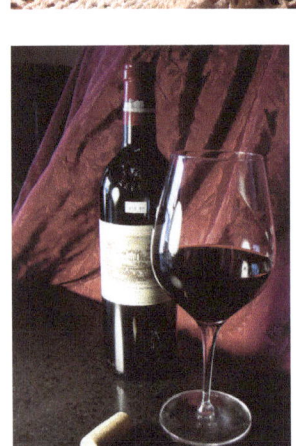

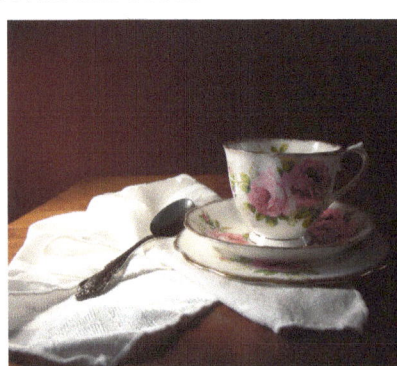

Planning Your Composition

Even though you did a lot of work on your composition at the setup stage, there is still a little more work to do. The more thoroughly you work out the details beforehand the more fun your painting process will be. Whatever problems you neglect to work out at this stage will haunt you throughout the painting.

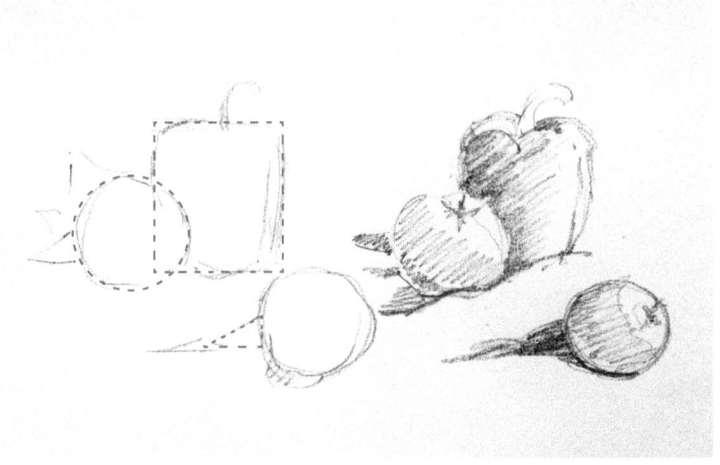

All objects can be reduced to the most basic shapes: circle, square, and triangle. From those basic shapes we can add shading and distortion to make cones, rectangles, cylinders, ovals, and so on. These simple shapes are found everywhere.

Try to sketch the most basic shapes (triangles, cones, squares, ovals, etc.) from your composition in your sketchbook. Place the objects in a pleasing way on your paper. Don't worry about any details until the basic shapes are in the correct places.

Now you will develop some thumbnail sketches from your basic shapes. Thumbnail sketches should be small and should be used for problem solving before you ever touch your watercolor paper. They are quick, sketchy little drawings of the basic shapes you are looking at. Thumbnails help you to quickly move objects around your picture plane, work on value contrast and develop a basic composition for your painting.

Remember to minimize the shapes to help you work quickly. This is not a final drawing, just a method to work out the most important aspects of your painting: composition and value. If your composition and values are right, your painting will be a success.

Things to think about while developing thumbnail sketches:
• Do I want to make this painting in a horizontal or vertical format?
• Do I want all of the objects to appear in whole or do I want to cut some off at the edges?
• How can I add more interest?
• Is this painting flat or are there interesting changes in plane,line and position?
• Where is my horizon line?
• What are the basic shapes of the objects I want to add to my painting?

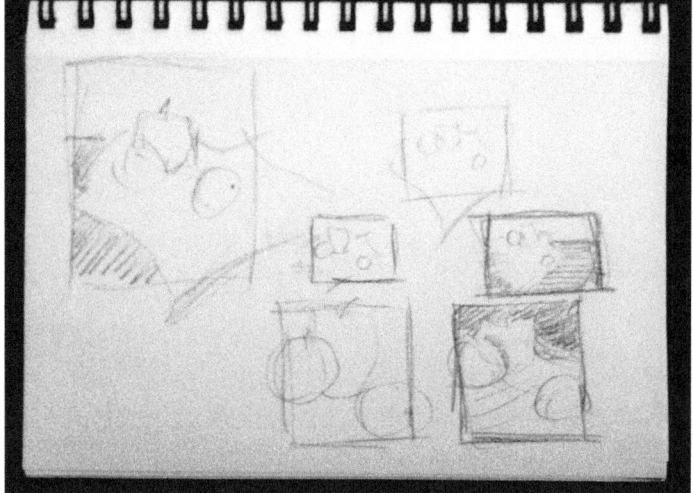

• How do the sizes of the shapes relate to one another?
• Are the distant objects smaller than the closer objects?
• How dark or light are the objects compared to each other?
• Where do I want the focal point or point of interest in my painting to be?
• How can I draw the viewers interest to the focal point? Use details, color, value contrast?
• Is this a subject that will keep me interested the entire timeI work on it?
• What details can I leave out of this piece?
• What details are essential to the piece?
• Is this painting telling a story, expressing an idea, telling something about the artist, or simply being painted for the pleasure of painting?
• Is there a dominant color in the painting?
• Are the colors leaning toward cool or warm?
• Is there a strong sense of light and dark to define the volume of the shapes?

Thumbnail Sketch Process

1. Look for the basic shapes in your composition.
   - Is it a triangle shape, a round shape, a rectangular shape?
   - Is it bigger on top than on the bottom?
   - Is it pear-shaped?
   - Is it soft-edged, crisp, or angular?
   - Are some objects overlapping?
   - Are there spaces between objects?
   - What shapes are the "empty" areas?
   - Where does the focal area fall in the picture plane?
     (Hint: draw a grid to help locate specific elements and get their relationship to one another correct.)

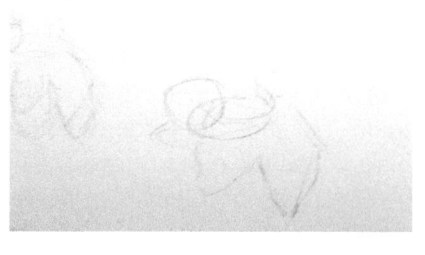

2. After capturing the basic outer shape of the objects, and their placement on the picture plane, ask yourself the same questions from step 1 about the individual parts: shadow shapes, cup handles, folds in fabric, and so on. Also ask yourself:
   - Do the objects reach up or swing out and down?
   - Are they close together or is there a bit of space between them?
   - Is there a crisp edge to the shadow shape or does it gently grade from dark to light?
   - Are the shapes correctly sized compared to each other?

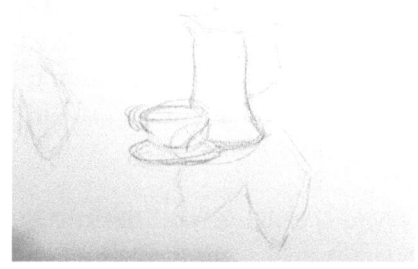

3. Now think in values.
   - Use your value scale* and think light = value 1; dark = value 6.
   - Mark the numbers 1 – 6 on your thumbnail to relate to the values.
   - If you have combined photo references for a better composition, decide the values for the added elements.
   - Pay attention to areas in shadow and in light.
   - Shade in the values according to your numbers with a pencil.

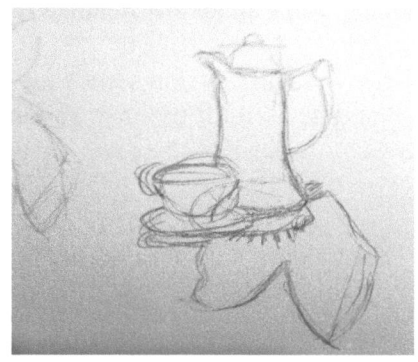

*A value scale is available in the reference photos section in this book.

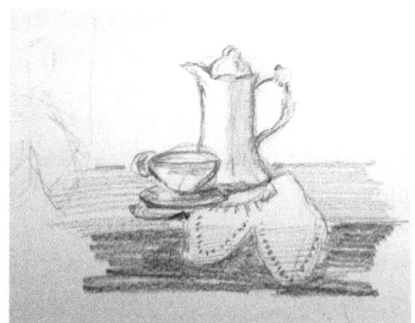

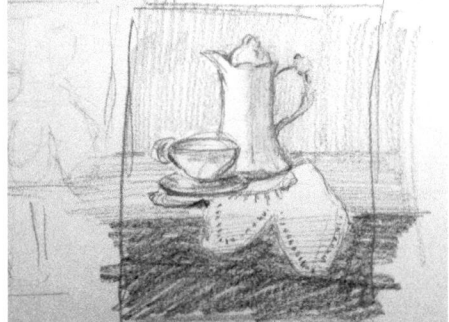

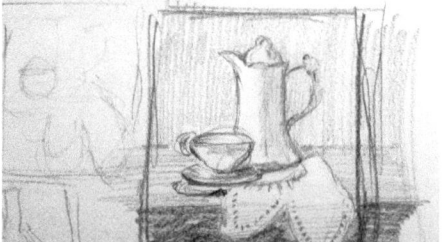

Thumbnail sketches are not final drawings. They are simply a method to work out solutions to common composition and value problems. Focus not on drawing but on the most basic elements of the picture.

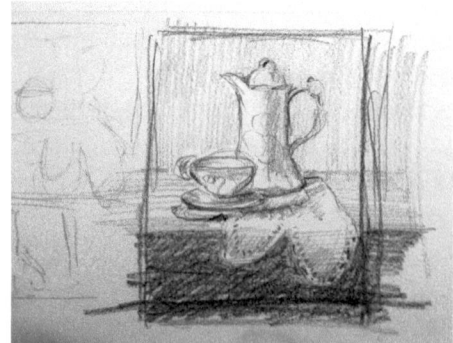

Preparing a Drawing

There are lots of ways to develop drawings for your paintings. Once you have developed a thumbnail sketch that you think fits your goals for the painting you can then make a larger drawing to match the size of your desired finished painting. Transfer this drawing to your watercolor paper.

Many of my students don't enjoy the drawing process as much as painting or simply don't have strong drawing skills, so I help them find simpler, easier ways to develop their drawings. Many fine, professional watercolor artists use slides or computers to help them in this process. Others use a grid system, which works very well. Others simply rely on the basics in their thumbnail sketches to get the simple ideas down, and then paint in a looser fashion, not worrying about the details at all.

If you have strong drawing skills, producing the drawing by hand from your references and thumbnails is the best approach. If you are anxious to paint or don't have strong drawing skills, you can make a small drawing by tracing your photos over a light box or by holding them up to a brightly lit window. Then, when you have the basic shapes and some of the details you want to capture in your drawing you can use a photocopier to enlarge the components and place them on the proper size drawing paper for your desired painting.

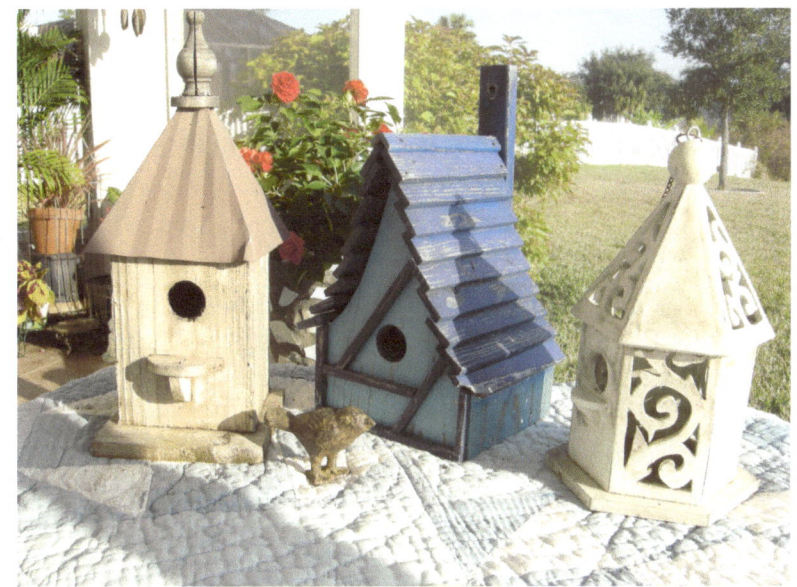

No matter how you prepare your drawing, make sure you develop it through sketching and study; this is crucial to a successful painting. This is the stage where you work out the road map for your painting. Take the time to sketch and get intimately familiar with the shapes and values of all the objects you want in your painting. You may even want to develop small watercolor sketches of the piece to work out color problems that may arise.

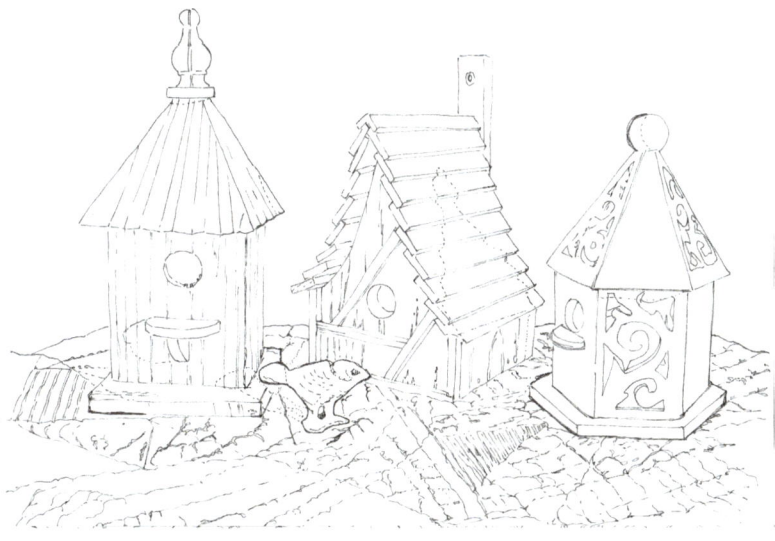

Now that you have a developed drawing, let's transfer it to your prepared watercolor paper. Remember, the drawing should be the exact size of the desired finished painting, or the same size as your watercolor sheet.

How to Prepare Watercolor Paper

What you will need:

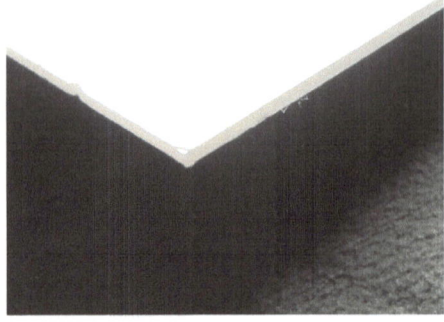

- Foam core board at least three inches bigger than your watercolor paper on all sides.
- Clear packing tape
- Two-inch wide masking tape
- Scissors
- Watercolor paper

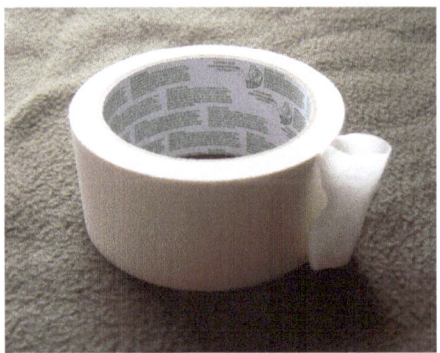

Some artists stretch wet paper onto heavy boards to keep the sheets flat while painting. I prefer the simple method of mounting dry paper onto foam core board to maintain the integrity of my paper while painting.

The process that I use protects the areas of the foam core board where you will eventually tape your watercolor paper. The clear packing tape prevents the masking tape from tearing the foam core and it slightly waterproofs the edges to protect it when applying juicy washes onto your painting. This board, if properly prepared, will be useful for many paintings in the future. It is a lightweight alternative to traditional watercolor paper stretching.

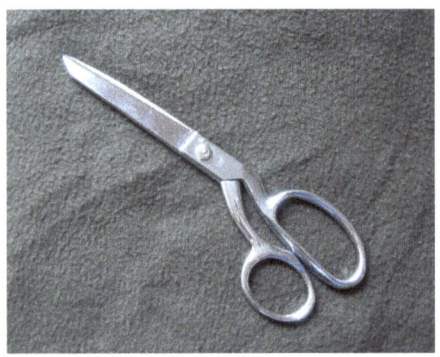

1. Cut the foam core board so that it measures about two inches larger than your watercolor paper on all sides.

2. Tape the outer edges of the foam core with clear packing tape. Cover the edges with at least two rows of tape on all sides, front and back. This board may be used over and over again as a support for your watercolor paper.

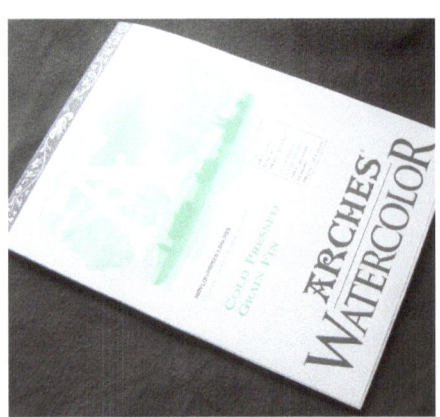

Tape watercolor paper to prepared foam core board with masking tape. Be sure that at least one half inch of your watercolor paper is covered with the tape to secure it to the board. Remember, your paper will get wet while painting. This will cause it to buckle, warp and stretch. The secure application of tape will hold it firmly to the foam core during the painting process.

Your framer will appreciate the fact that your artwork was stretched to stay flat. Framing a warped or bowed watercolor is very difficult.

Now you are ready to transfer a drawing to your paper.

Transfer the Drawing to Watercolor Paper

What you will need:
• Watercolor paper
• Completed drawing and thumbnail sketches
• Photo references
• Chunky graphite stick
• Pencil for tracing
• Prepared foam core stabilizer board
• Two-inch-wide masking tape

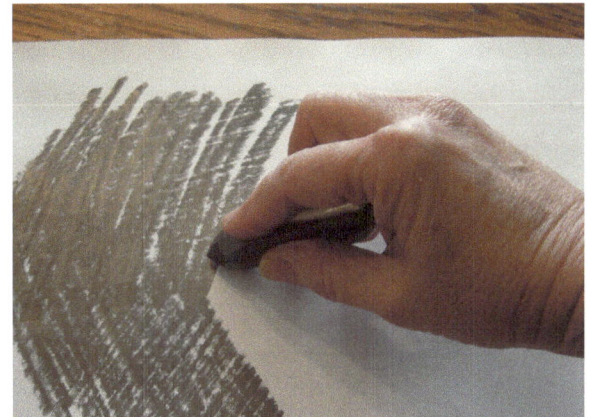

1. Scrub the chunky graphite stick on the back of your completed drawing. Use a little elbow grease to get good coverage over the entire image area.

2. Use a tissue to gently smooth over the graphite to release loose crumbs and to fill in the spaces where the graphite didn't completely cover the paper. Use a light touch.

3. Wash your hands! This will keep your watercolor paper clean.

4. Use a strip of masking tape and secure the drawing on one edge to your watercolor paper, like a hinge. This will allow you to lift the drawing occasionally to check your progress, without losing your alignment.

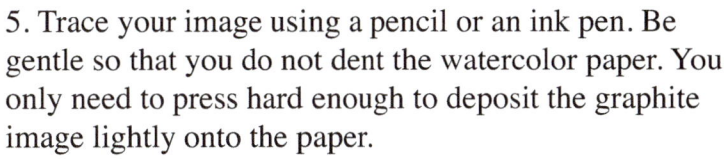
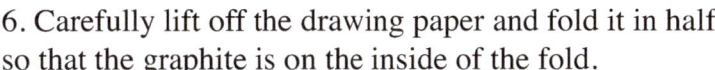

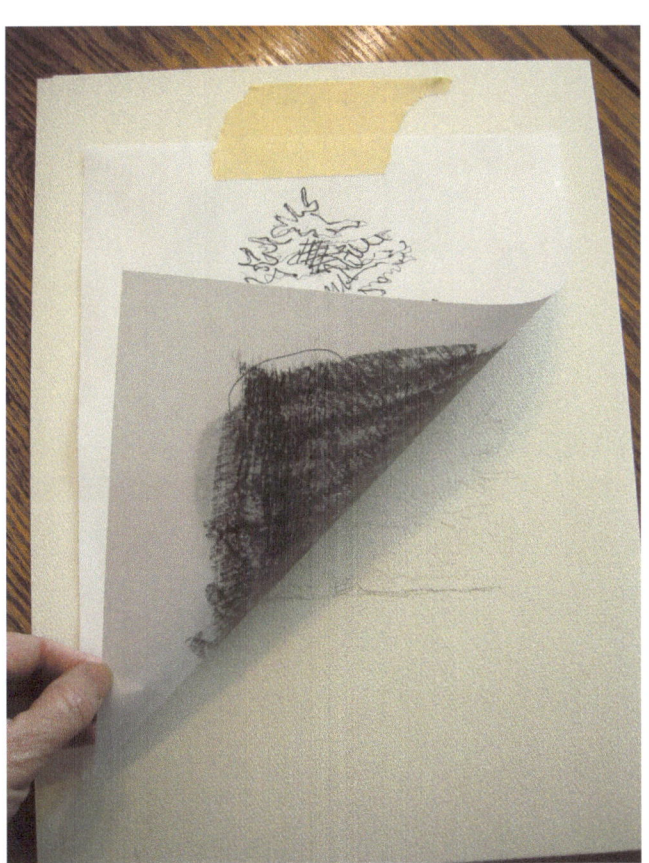

5. Trace your image using a pencil or an ink pen. Be gentle so that you do not dent the watercolor paper. You only need to press hard enough to deposit the graphite image lightly onto the paper.

6. Carefully lift off the drawing paper and fold it in half so that the graphite is on the inside of the fold.

7. Now you can use a pencil to correct any markings you may want to fix. Using a white vinyl eraser you may also gently erase places where you don't want the graphite.

8. Place your watercolor paper on the prepared foam core board. Secure it with the masking tape. Be sure to cover at least one half inch of the paper edges with the tape to keep it from buckling when wet. Now you are ready to paint!

An alternative method is to use graphite transfer paper purchased from an art supply store.

Masking

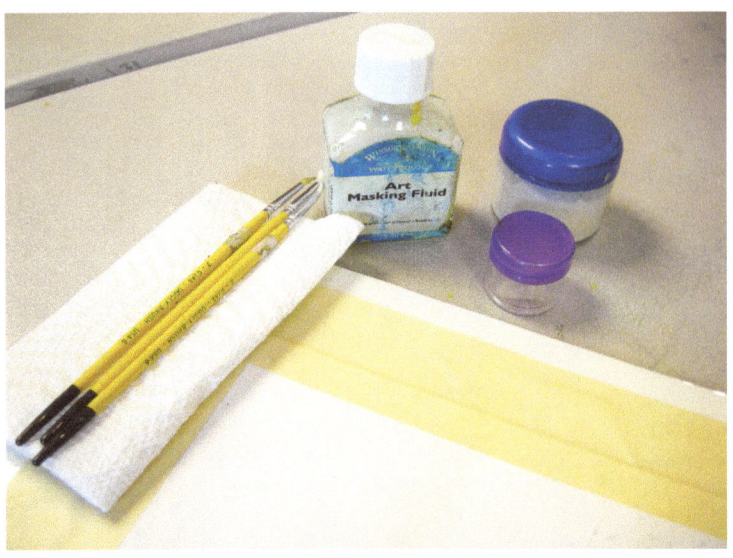

After tracing your drawing onto your watercolor paper, mask the white areas of the painting. Go slowly and use thought in your marks. You will be stuck with what you have so treat this as "painting your whites". Only mask the white areas that you do not want pigment to touch. You will paint around some of the other white areas.

I use Winsor & Newton Yellow-Tinted masking fluid and a small, fine point brush coated with soapy water. The two containers shown here are so handy! I use one to hold some thick, soapy water. You can use dish soap, or a small piece of bar-type soap (plain, like Ivory) and a little water. The water softens the soap but leaves it thick so it will adhere well to your brush, protecting it from the very destructive-to-brushes masking fluid.

I pour a small amount of masking fluid into the smaller jar so that I do not have to keep the main jar of masking fluid open. It dries out and thickens quickly. I only pour out what I think I need for the current project.

I have dedicated brushes for masking. I like to use the brushes that are designed for masking. They have a firm bristle and may be purchased in several sizes for details or covering large areas.

Never mix your masking tools with your regular painting tools. Use different water, paper towels, and so on. Masking will ruin your good brushes, so keep them completely separate.

You can also use a very cheap little brush for masking. I coat the brush with thick, soapy water and then dip just a little masking at a time. I keep dipping into the thick, soapy mixture in between applications of masking to preserve the brush as much as possible. If an area to be masked is extremely small, I sometimes use a toothpick to apply the masking.

Don't use a hot hair dryer on your masking as this will "bake" the masking into your watercolor paper and make it difficult to remove.

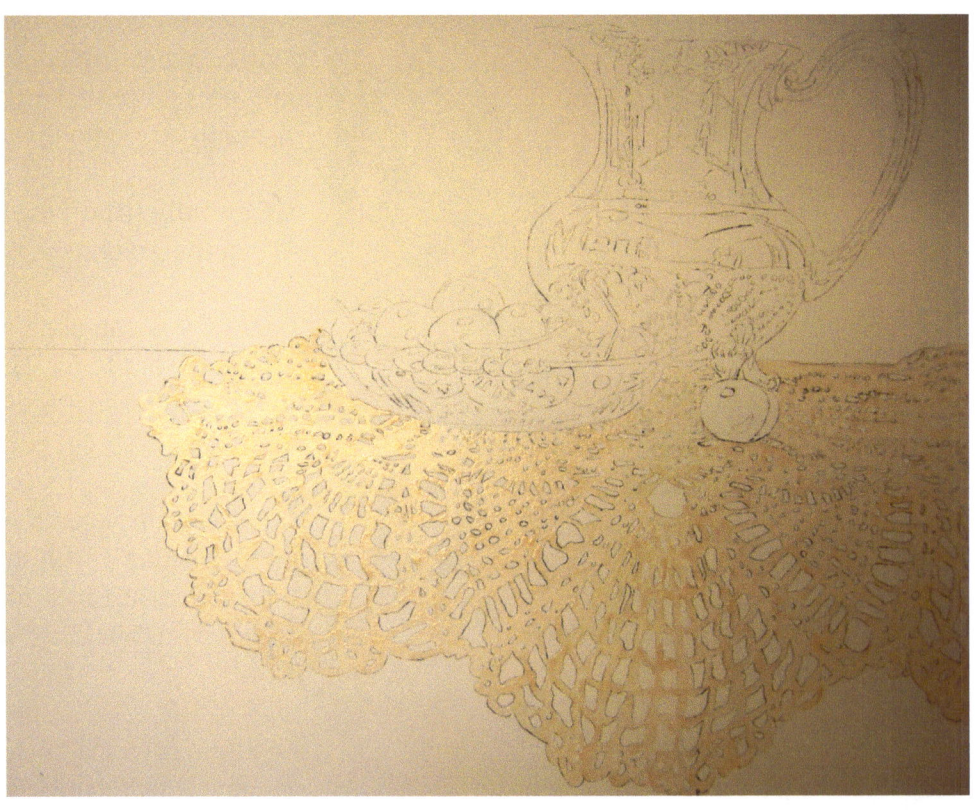

Painting Silver and Cherries

At this point you should have a drawing applied to watercolor paper, the paper should be properly applied to a stable surface such as a foam core board, and any white areas that you desire to preserve should be masked. I masked the doily only for this painting.

Background

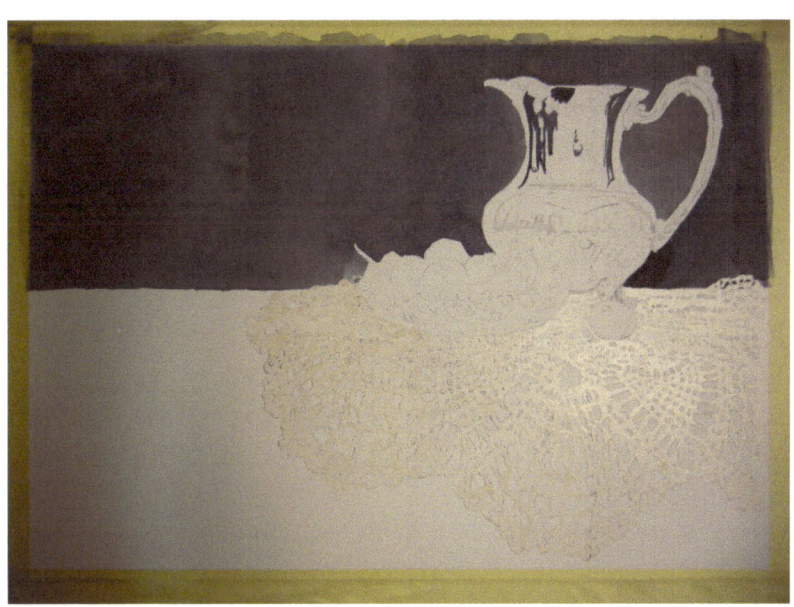

You want to have some drama on the stage of this painting, so go for a very dark background wash. I created a big flat wash here (one solid tone). I physically mixed Burnt Sienna and French Ultramarine Blue on the palette, producing a strong color, that was wet enough to flow nicely (see Review of Basic Painting Skills for instructions on laying in a flat wash).

Paint a flat wash in the background around the pitcher. Then, when that area is complete, paint the same wash inside the handle.

Double-Check Values (lights and darks)

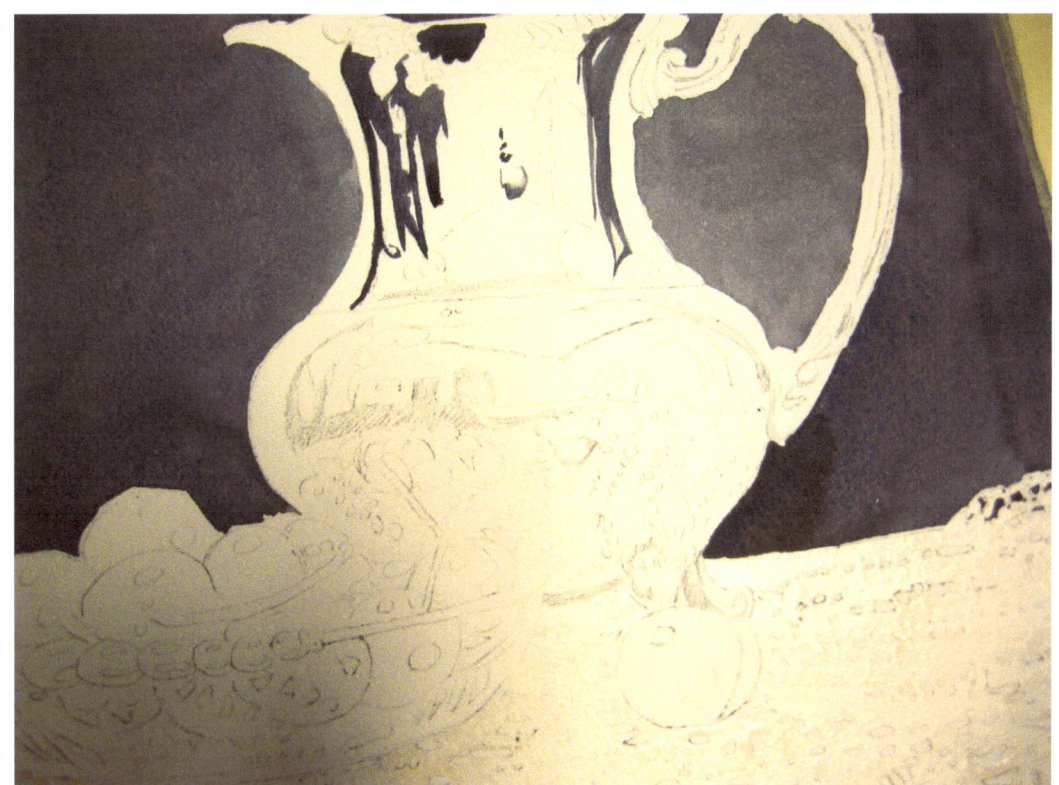

Use a pencil and look carefully at your photo reference. Mark in the darkest values by lightly drawing in the value directly onto your painting. This will help you to navigate through the painting.

There are a lot of complicated, abstract shapes that represent the world that is reflected by the shiny, mirror surface of the pitcher. Think about penciling in only the very darkest values. Simplify the shapes as much as you can, but keep the basic shapes accurate to your reference. Look for the items in the room that will be reflected there: a doorway, windows, the lace, and so on. Notice that the same things are reflected in several areas of the pitcher due to its curved shape.

Make a big puddle of Burnt Sienna on your palette. This should be a light tea or coffee valued mixture – use lots of water!

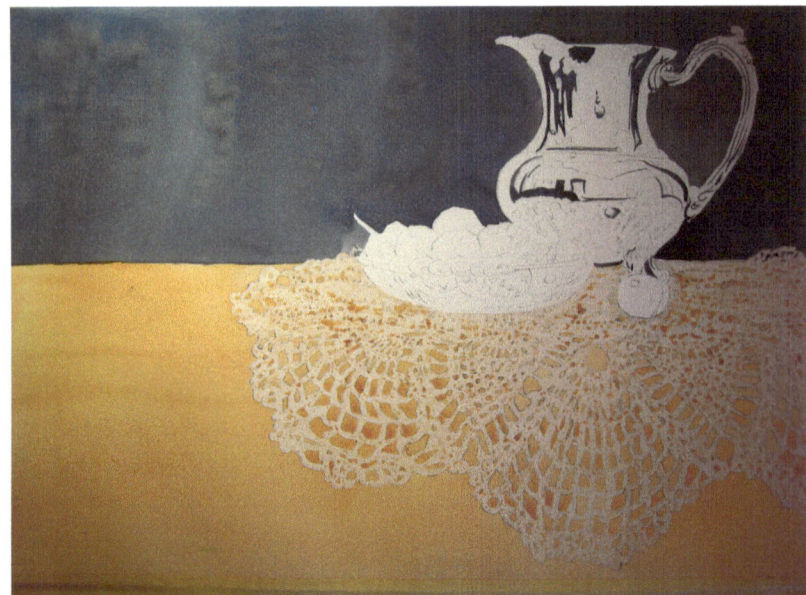

Wash this mixture over the table. Keep it light and wet. Any brushwork that may show should run horizontally! If you work very wet you can apply the wash vertically, then tip and turn to allow gravity to blend and smooth it out. Avoid the temptation to use your brush to smooth out a wash. This is where the time you took to mask the lacy doily comes in so handy. You can wash directly over the mask, being careful not to use pressure on your brush. Pressure will not only pull up some of the masked edges; it will also ruin your wash by leaving brush marks on the fragile watercolor paper.

Use Winsor Red to create a light, tea stain wash on the cherries. Keep it light! We'll add more details later. You can vary the wash so that it is more graded than flat, but don't overwork it or you will spoil what comes later. Paint around the highlighted areas for now.
Don't forget the little wisp of red that is reflected in the glass at the bottom of the bowl.

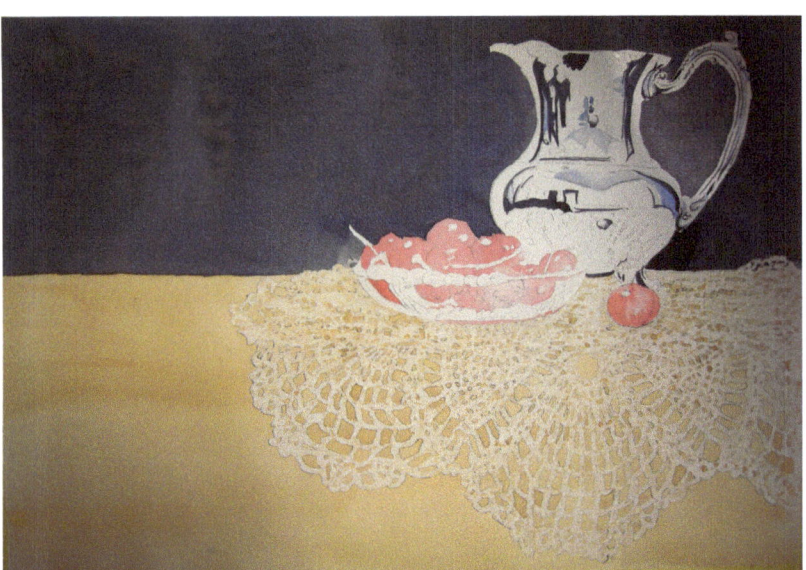

Use French Ultramarine Blue to create some very light, reflected cool areas in the pitcher. Look carefully at your photo references. Don't put in too much information. Be very selective in your application. Also be aware that most edges are crisp, but some are soft, especially where the vessel bends and rounds toward the background. This is a great location to play with graded washes (dark to light).

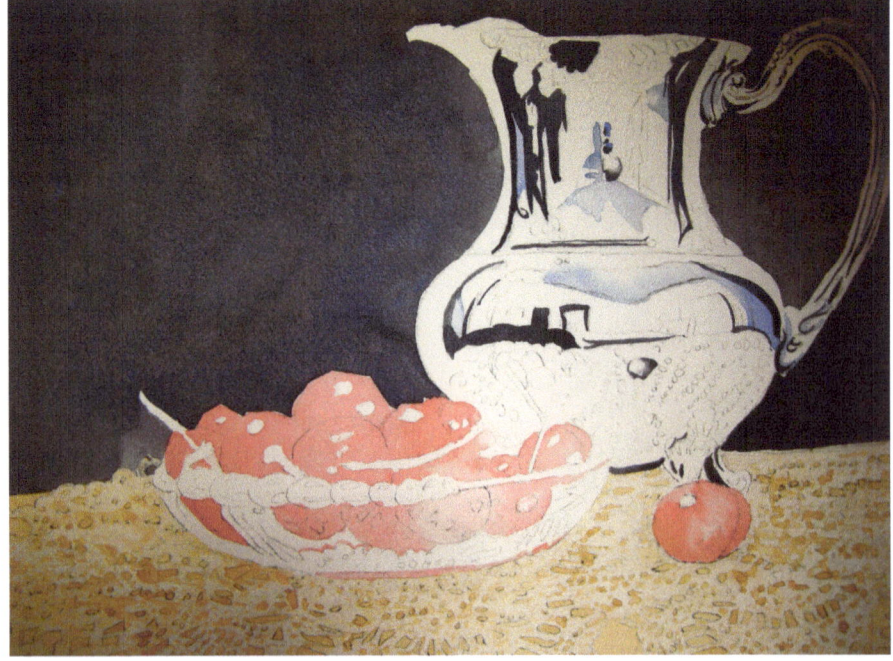

Time for some wet-in-wet!
Have your French Ultramarine Blue
and Permanent Alizarin Crimson
moist and ready to go. We want the
paint to have about a 50-50 ratio
of water to pigment consistency,
because we will be diluting the
pigments into the wet areas of the
pitcher.

Wet the pitcher with clear water at
the bottom where you may notice
some very soft reflections. Drip in
two or three drops of each color – Do
not mix with your brush! Allow this
to just rest. It will blend on its own if
you have applied enough water in the
first place. In this photo you can see
the shine of my water and how deep it is.

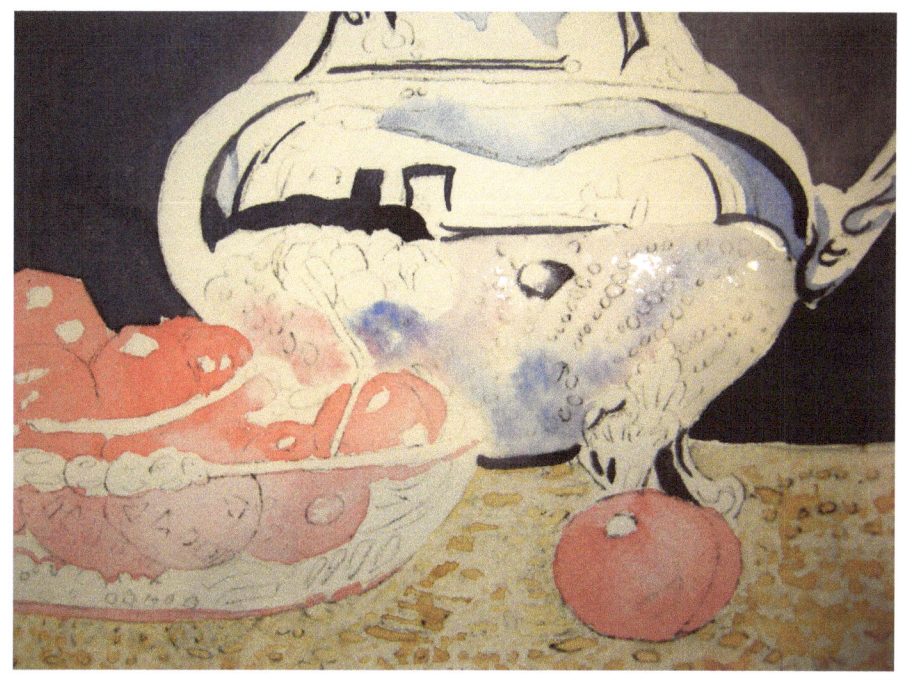

Create the same wet-in-wet wash
technique to the top of the pitcher
where it curves out and around and
at the very bottom of the glass dish.
Keep this light and airy. Don't work
it with a brush at all, just allow it to
blend on its own with the moisture already on the paper. If it isn't going as
fast as you would like, just gently tip
the board. Don't touch it with your
brush except to apply the water.

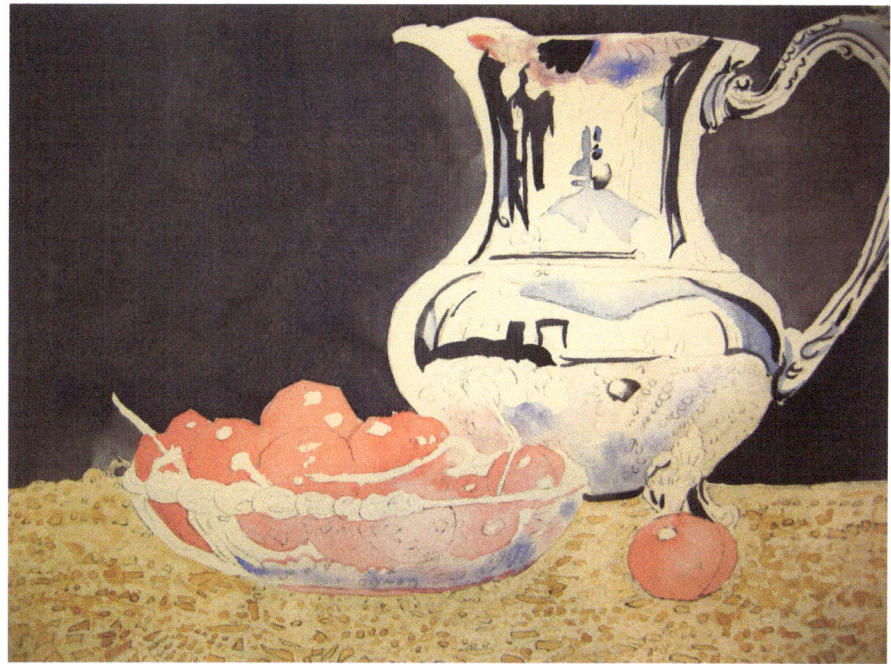

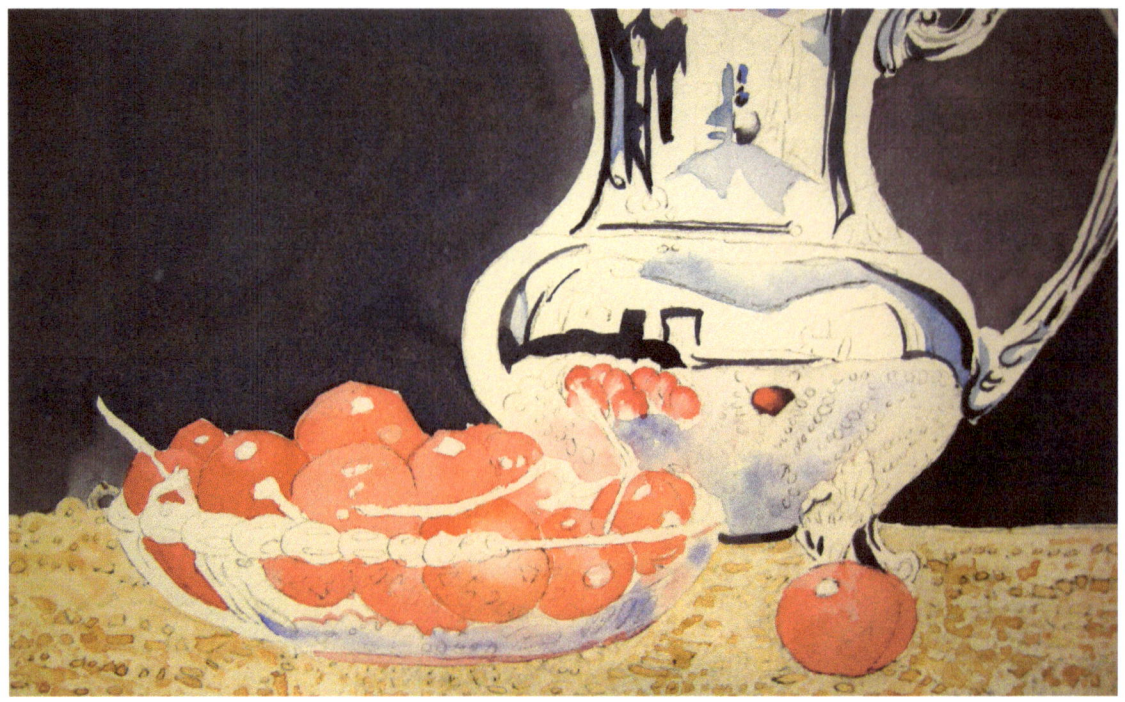

Since reflections are always darker than what they are reflecting, we want to use a cool red for the cherry reflections in pitcher. I chose Permanent Alizarin Crimson. Apply just a touch to the cherries in the pitcher. Paint one at a time, mostly the edges and create a soft edge in the center of each cherry by pushing a moist (not dripping wet) brush into the wash while it is still wet. Then move on to the next cherry. Be sure the areas next to what you are painting are completely dry in order to retain a crisp edge.

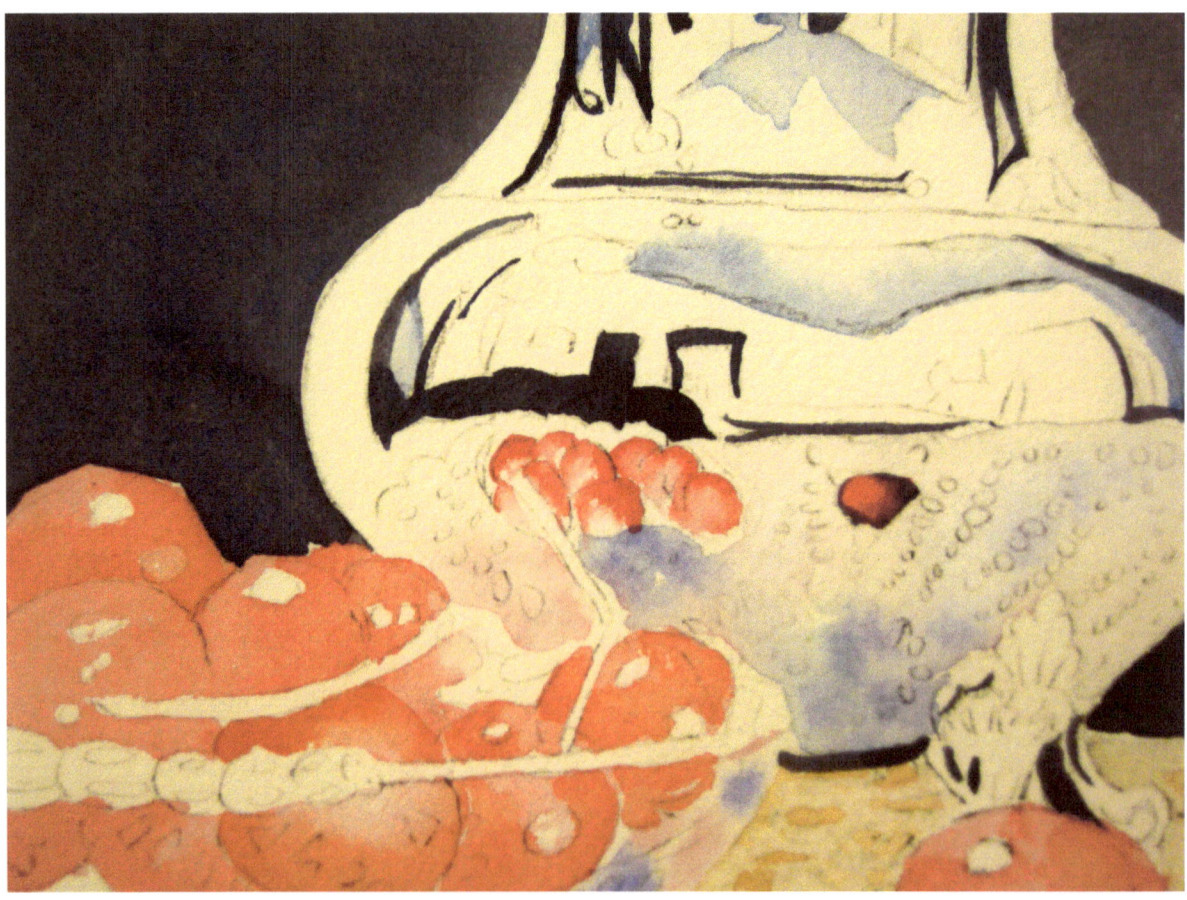

Here is a close-up view of what we have so far.

Use a pencil and a straight edge or ruler and draw a line across your painting that will indicate where the edge of the table is found. The table in the reference photo is a drop leaf table, so it is not deep. We want to create a shadow by painting a wash along the bottom edge of the table. Use the line to indicate where the plane of the table changes. I used a very wet mixture of Burnt Sienna and a little "mud" from my palette. You can use Burnt Sienna and a little touch of French Ultramarine Blue or whatever little puddle you may already have on your palette.

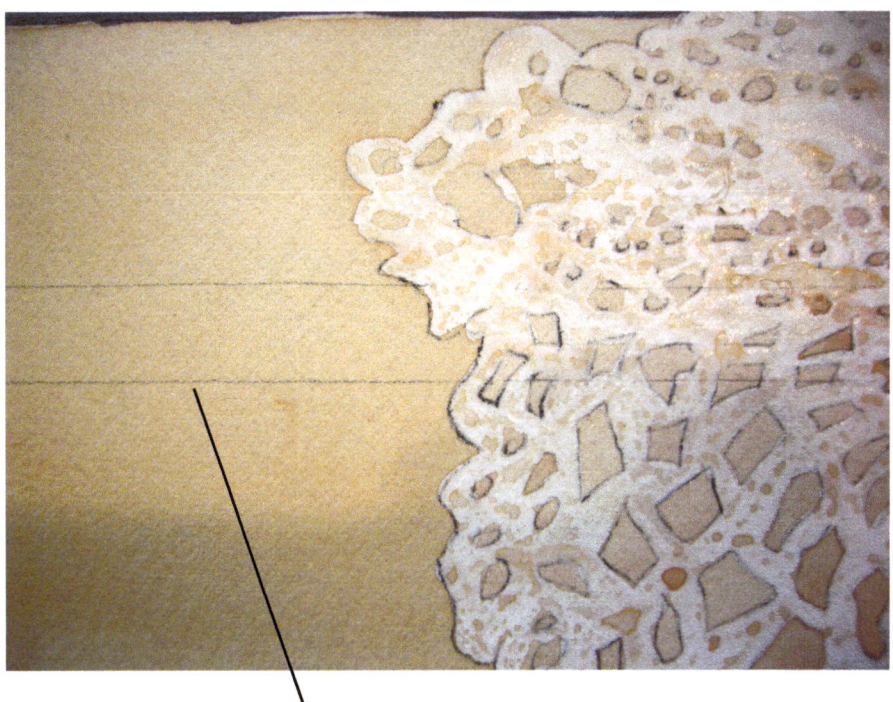

Paint a wash from here down and across.

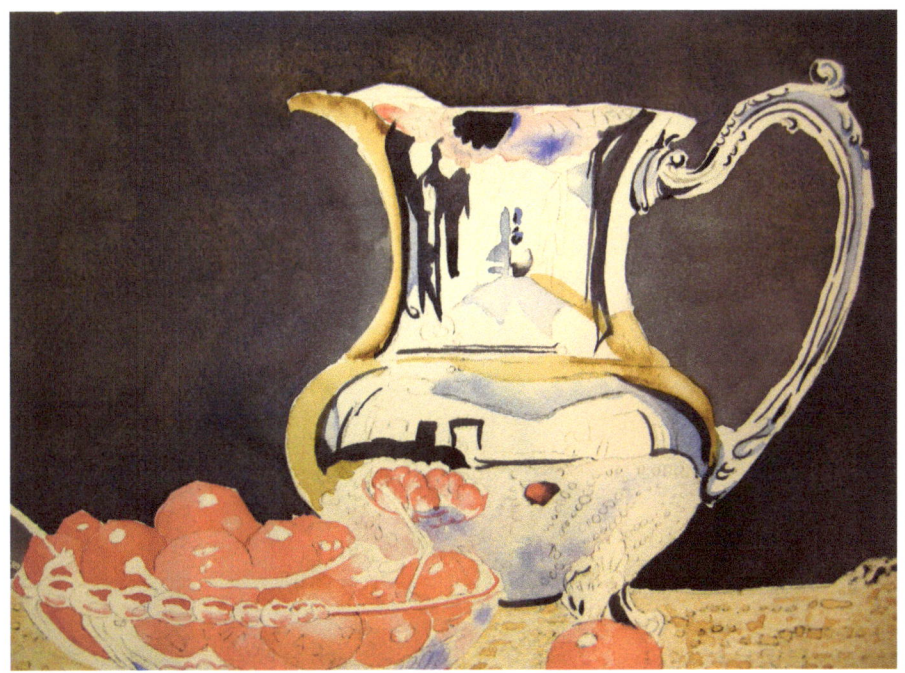

Here I have added some VanDyke Brown to my mud puddle (the one I used for the bottom, shadow area of the table). I have it loaded with water so that it is about a tea or weak coffee consistency. I applied this mixture to the sides of the pitcher, some in the center and a touch in the handle. Look carefully at your photo reference to see where it may be appropriate.

While the wash was still wet, I applied a touch of milk-consistency (thicker) VanDyke Brown to the areas that appeared darker to me in the reference photo (wet-in-wet technique). Notice the top of the spout, where a slight shadow is formed because it curves away from the reflected light, as well as the right side, near the bottom of the curve by the handle. Just a touch goes a long way. Just drop a small amount into the moist wash you already applied, and allow the wet pigment to blend on its own. Don't blend with a brush as this will get overworked and look dry.

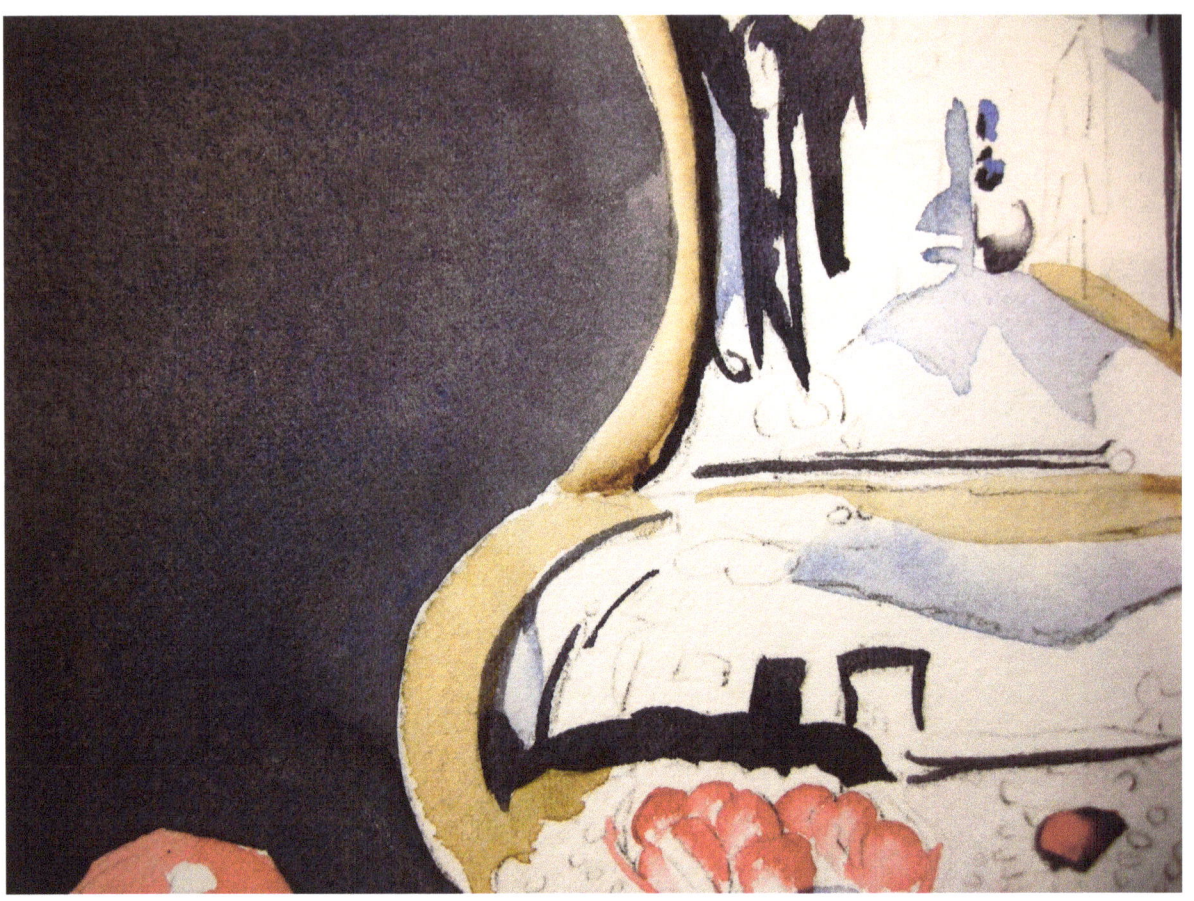

Okay, it is beginning to take shape! It looks pretty sloppy close up, but when you step back, which you should do often when you are painting, it looks much nicer. When you use simple strokes, and do not overwork your painting it will seem to have more life, sparkle, and vibrancy when viewed from a natural distance.

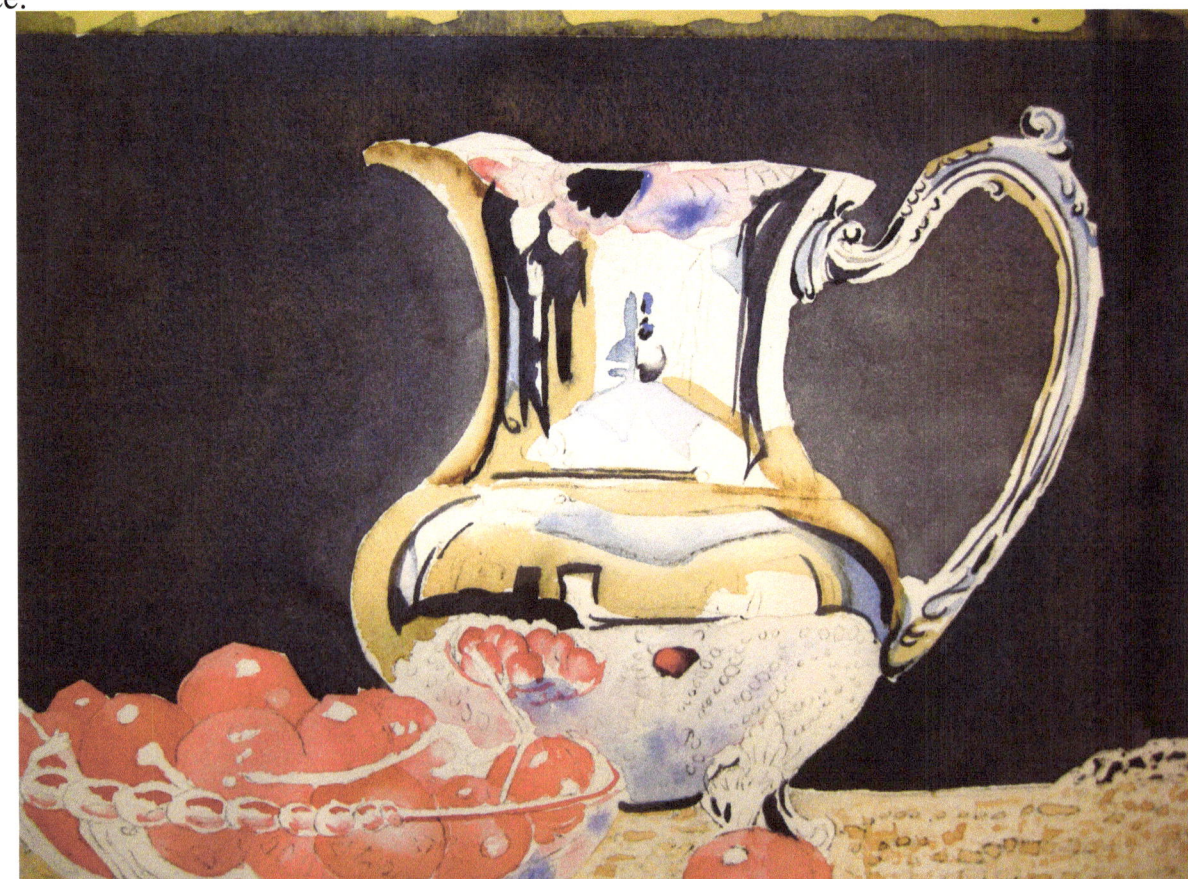

Wood Grain on the Table

To add wood grain details to the table use the push-pull stroke. You can see this technique in video format at: http://www.youtube.com/watercolorworks

Use large strokes at first to provide a hint of the grain. The details will come later. The edges can be simple and varied to add interest and to end up with a more believable texture.

To create a push-pull stroke, use a wet pigment and a round, pointed brush. I like to use my Number 10 round brush for this technique.

Hold the brush nearly straight up and down. Gently touch the paper

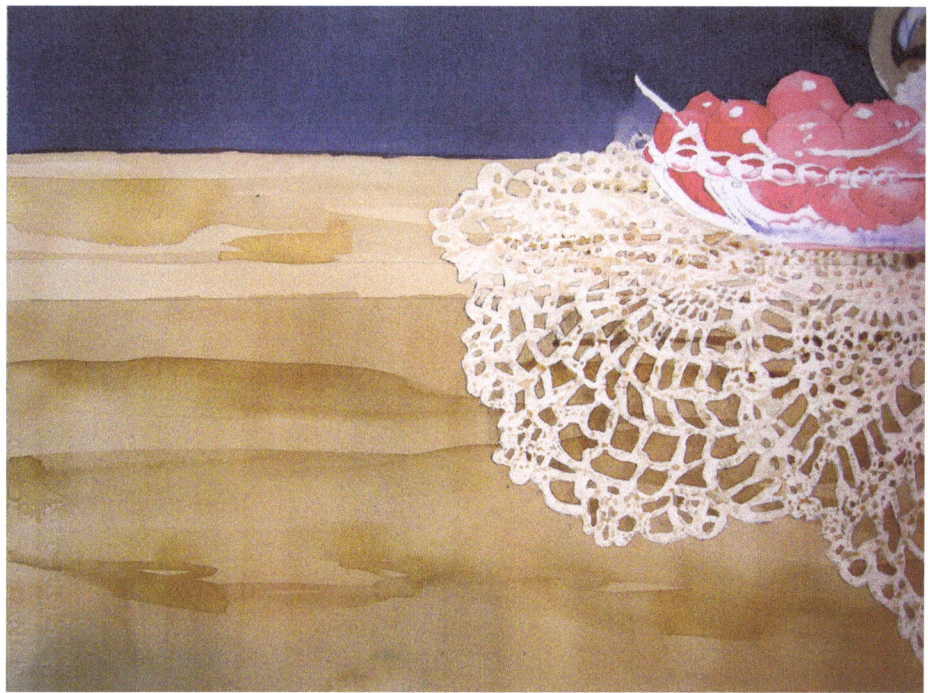

with your pigment and pull along in straight and zigzag strokes, varying the pressure as you pull it along. This creates a beautiful stroke!

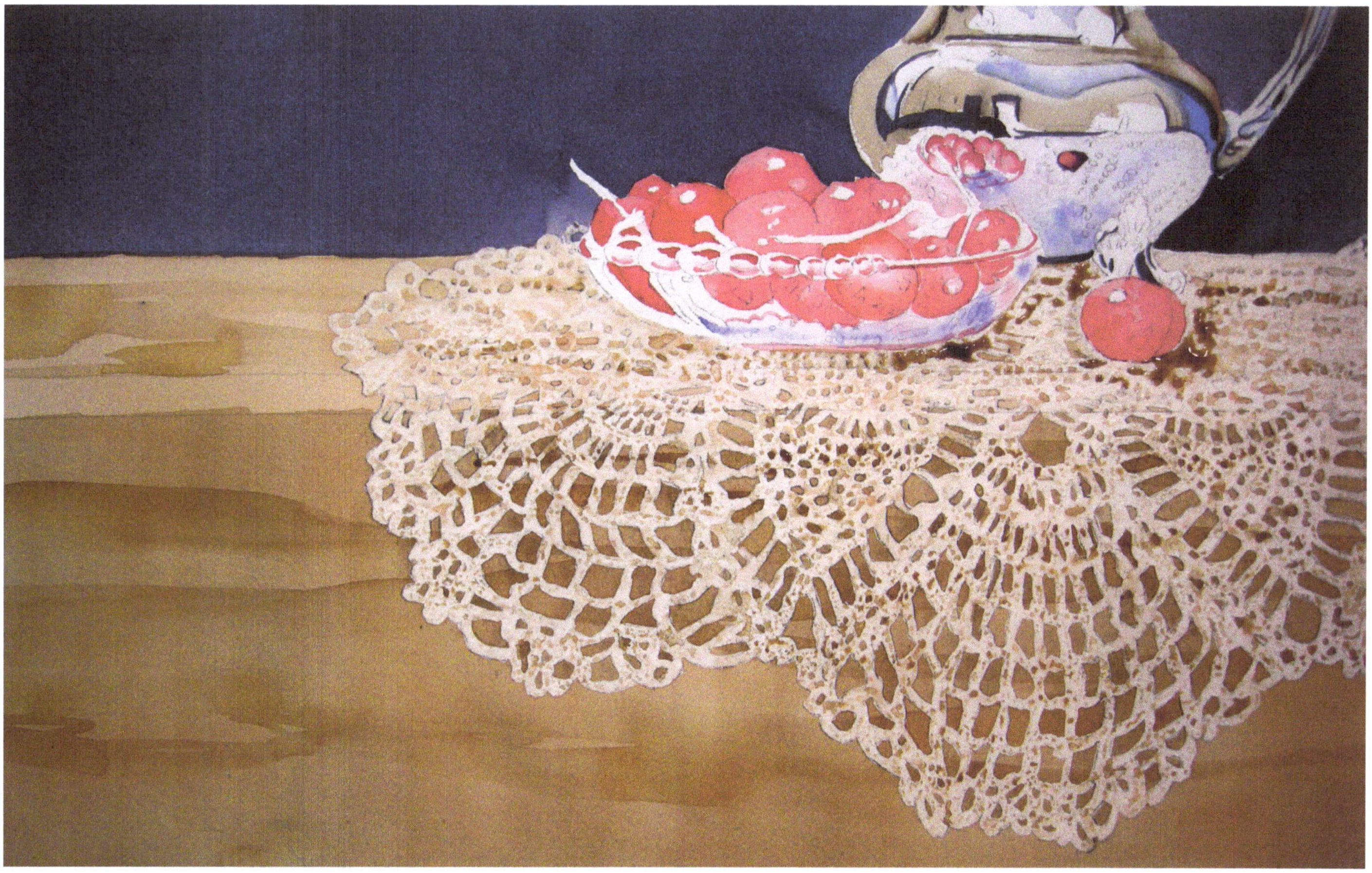

I used some of the cooler colors already on my palette to drop in some cast shadows under the doily. Use a wet pigment and be frugal. Too much will not look natural. Less is more is the theme here. Think ahead and look at your photo reference before you apply the pigment.

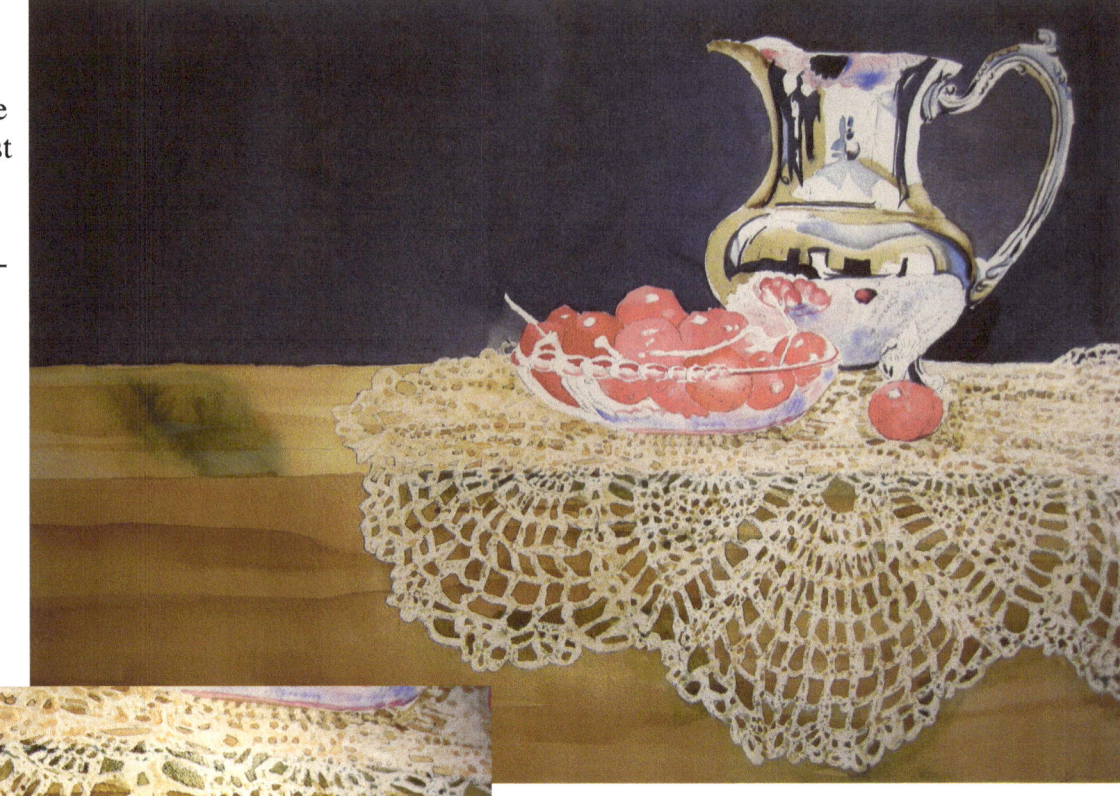

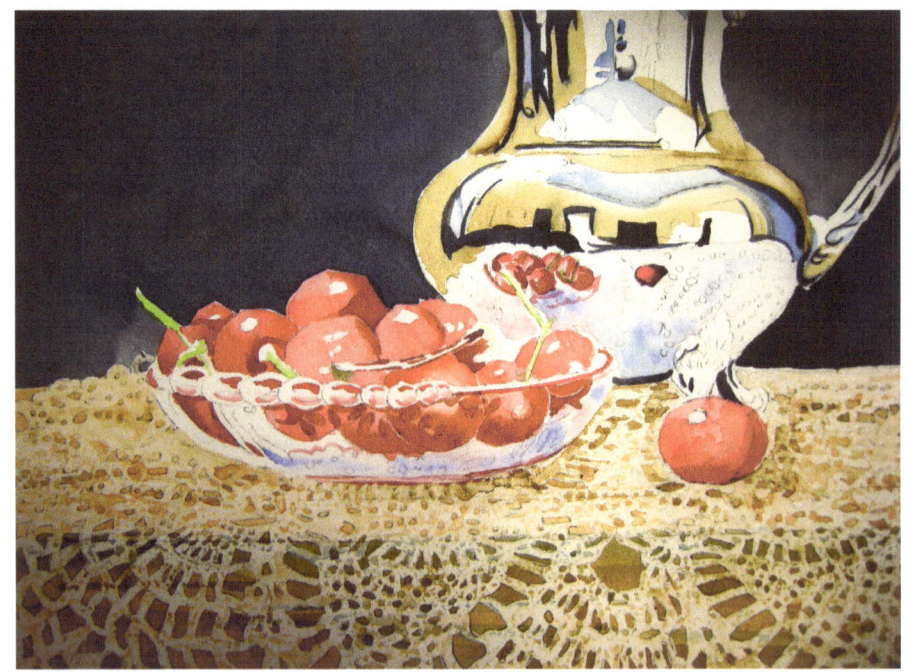

The stems of the cherries have been ignored until now. I used a little Sap Green and a touch of Burnt Sienna. The Burnt Sienna is great for the shadow areas of the stems. It also is good as a tiny, very wet wash over the dry green pigment to make it look less bright. Sap Green and Burnt Sienna are relative opposites on the color wheel. When using these colors to glaze (wet pigment over dried pigment) they will neutralize each other. We want natural, not gaudy.

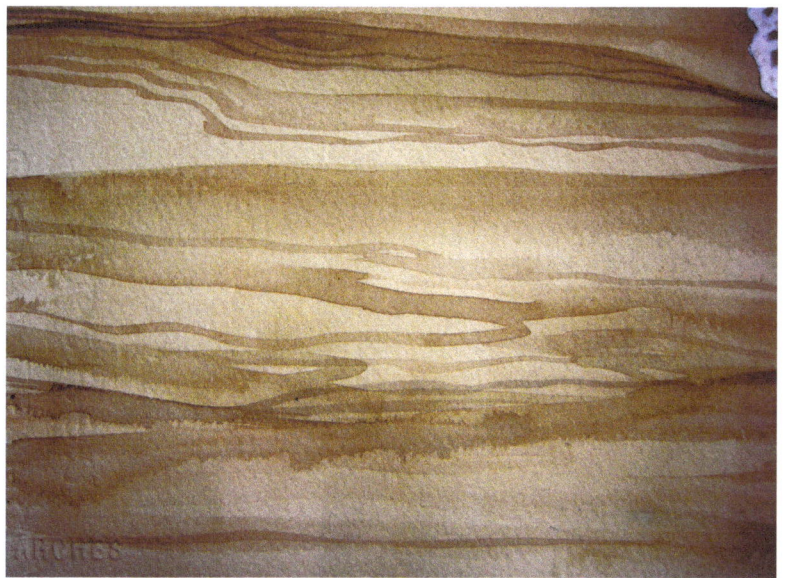

Adding more details to the wood grain involved applying the push-pull stroke again. This is a calligraphic stroke using very wet pigments. I applied a little squiggle of pigment with my Number 8 round brush. Then I quickly rinsed the brush, touched it to my paper towel and glided it along one edge of the wet stroke to soften the crisp edge with a little water. Be careful to not overdo this as it will begin to look fussy. Practice on a scrap piece of watercolor paper and watch my YouTube video for more detailed description of this technique.

We have a shadow where the plane of the table changes, but I wanted to describe the edge a bit more. I used a mixture of French Ultramarine Blue and Burnt Sienna to create this dark glaze. I used a softened-edge stroke for this area. Using a Number 12 round brush, I loaded the brush with a very wet mixture of the paint. I drew the brush along a few inches, using the tip of the brush to describe the crisp edge at the top of the edge of the table. I quickly rinsed the brush, touched the paper toweling, and ran the moist brush along the bottom edge of the stroke before it had a chance to dry. It is very important to brush any liquid into the stroke, and not out of the stroke. Pulling away from the original stroke will dilute and remove color, creating a dirty edge at the bottom. Pushing the liquid into the stroke will simply moisten and soften the edge without diluting the original stroke and it will create a graded edge from pure water (clear) to the full color of the stroke.

Allow the top area to dry. Then do the same stroke from bottom to top. This will preserve some of the original color of the table edge and yet describe the change of plane that becomes the side of the table.

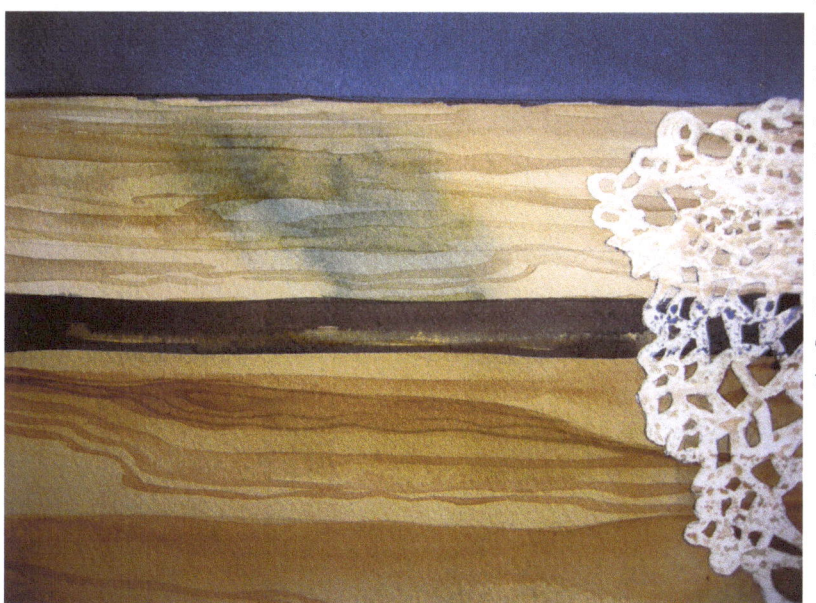

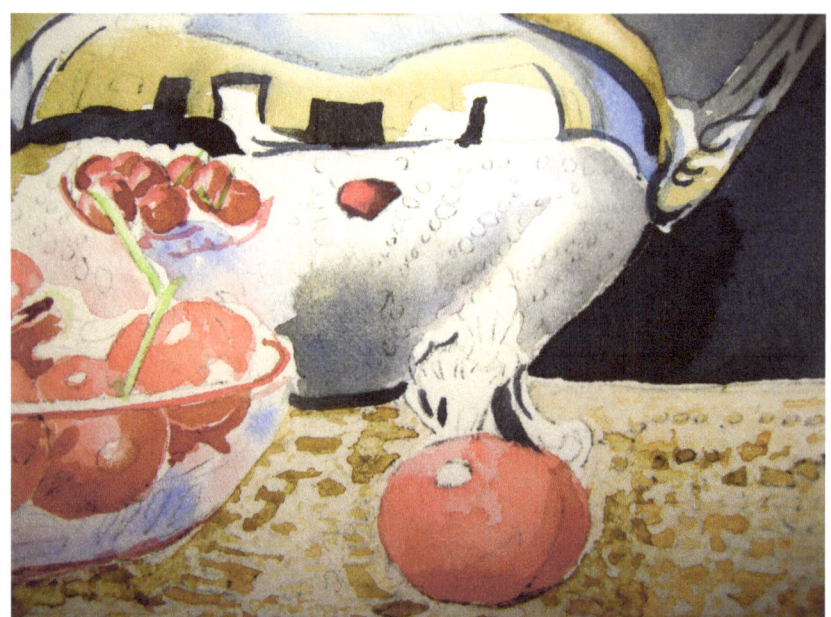

Here I added another cool red wash of Permanent Alizarin Crimson to the shadow of the cherries. Notice the separate cherry reflected in the silver pitcher. It has a much darker shadow where it faces the pitcher. A dark, warm brown like VanDyke Brown works well for this. Peryline Maroon would also make a good shadow color.

I diluted the VanDyke Brown and mixed it with some Quinacridone Gold to stipple in some shadowy areas around the doily.

I used VanDyke Brown and French Ultramarine Blue to create the wet, graded washes around the base of the silver pitcher.

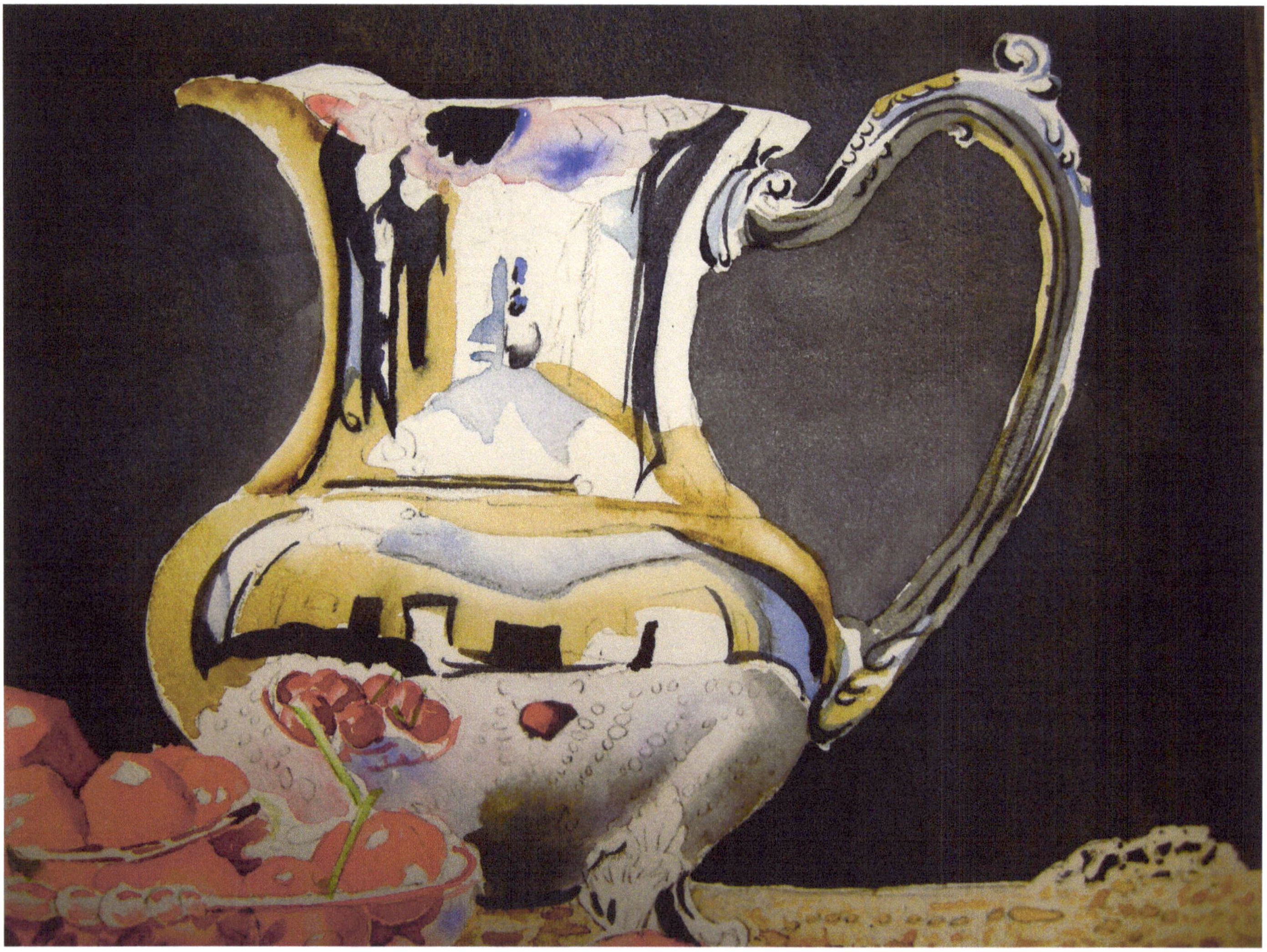

When adding details, remember less is more. Use simple strokes and avoid the temptation to continue brushing and playing with the pigment. Work hard to simply drop it in and let it go. This will keep it looking fresh.

Remove the Masking

I always love this stage of a painting! I use a masking pick-up tool for this task. Look for one at your favorite art supply store, or order one online from one of the companies listed in the back of this book.

The tool is designed to pick up the dried masking without damaging your paper or smudging the pigments. Gently rub the tool over the dried mask and it will roll into an edge that can easily be lifted off. Gently touch the paper to be sure all of the masking was removed. Avoid touching the paper too much as this will leave oil marks from your skin

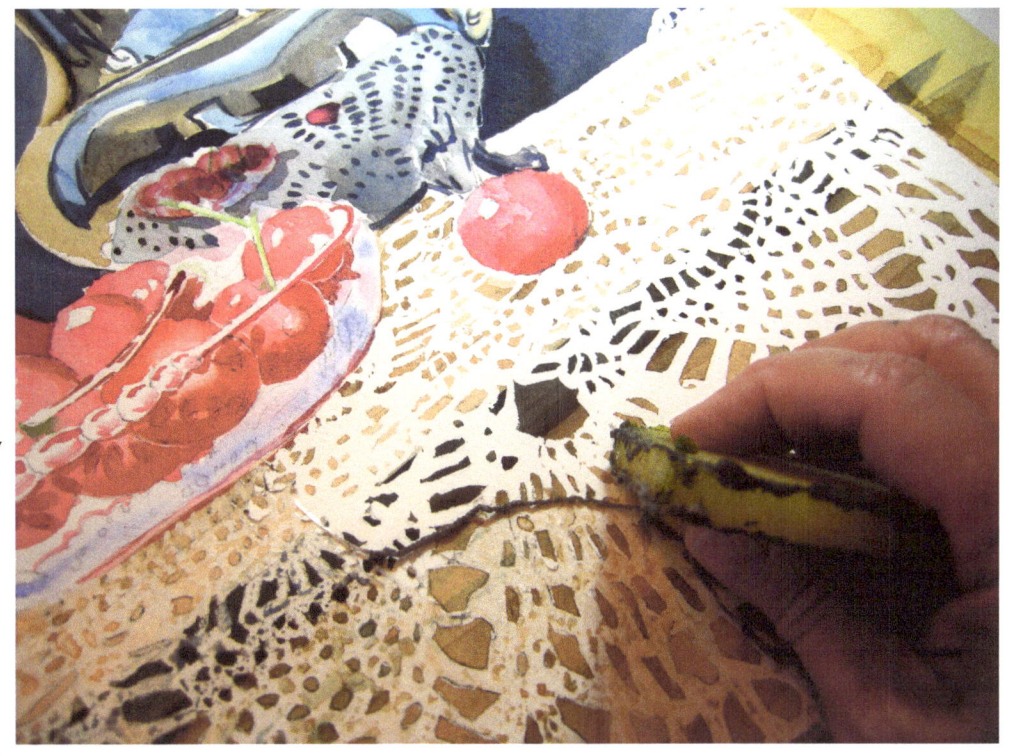

on the paper. Oil on your paper can affect future applications of paint and collect dust and dirt as the finished painting ages.

If the tool gets too dirty to work properly, simple trim the dirty edges from the tool with sharp scissors.

At this point I looked over every area of my painting and made notes regarding what finishing touches were still required.

I decided to add a few more washes to the silver pitcher. Look carefully at the shapes, lights and darks, and colors. Remember to keep things simple. The viewers eye will delight in seeing basic reflections. The viewers mind will put things together, and that is what makes a good painting engaging and a joy to view.

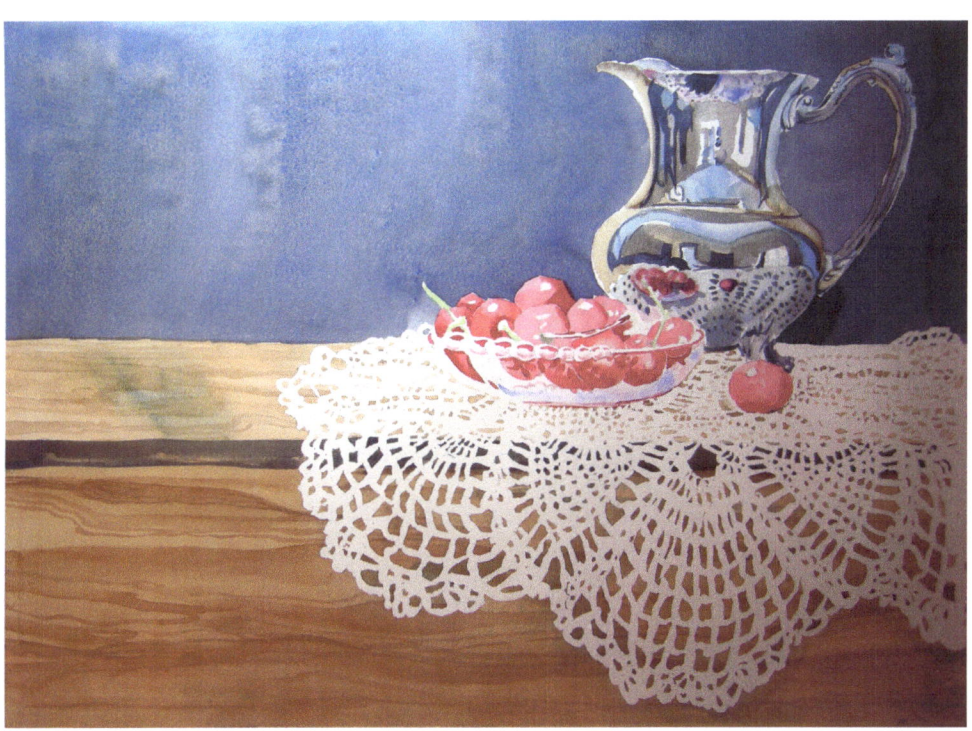

Shading the Doily

One of the items on my list was to add some shadows to the doily. The doily is not a flat object, so it should show areas where the light hits, and other areas where it is in shadow and casting shadows.

I used a mixture of French Ultramarine Blue and Burnt Sienna. In some areas I used more of the blue; in other areas where I wanted a warmer look, I used more Burnt Sienna.

Keep the washes very wet, using lots of water and very little pigment.

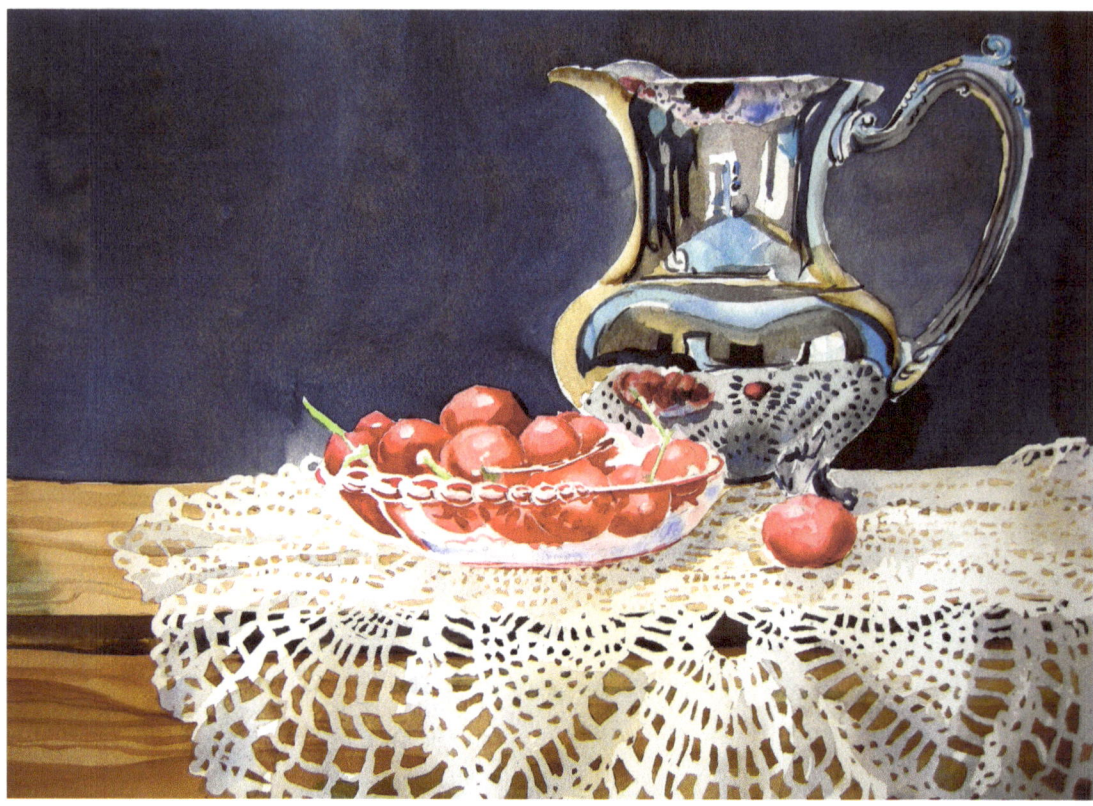

The goal here is to create the illusion of shadow very softly. I didn't want my shadows to take center stage. Soft edges are going to play a big role here. More crisp edges will draw the eye, so they are used more in the silver pitcher. Softer and more subtle areas will work more like props on the stage for the main characters to play against.

The closer the shadow is to an object, the darker the cast area of the shadow will be. As the shadow works away from the object it becomes lighter in value and softer in edge.

Step back and view your work from a distance. This is how most people will see your painting.

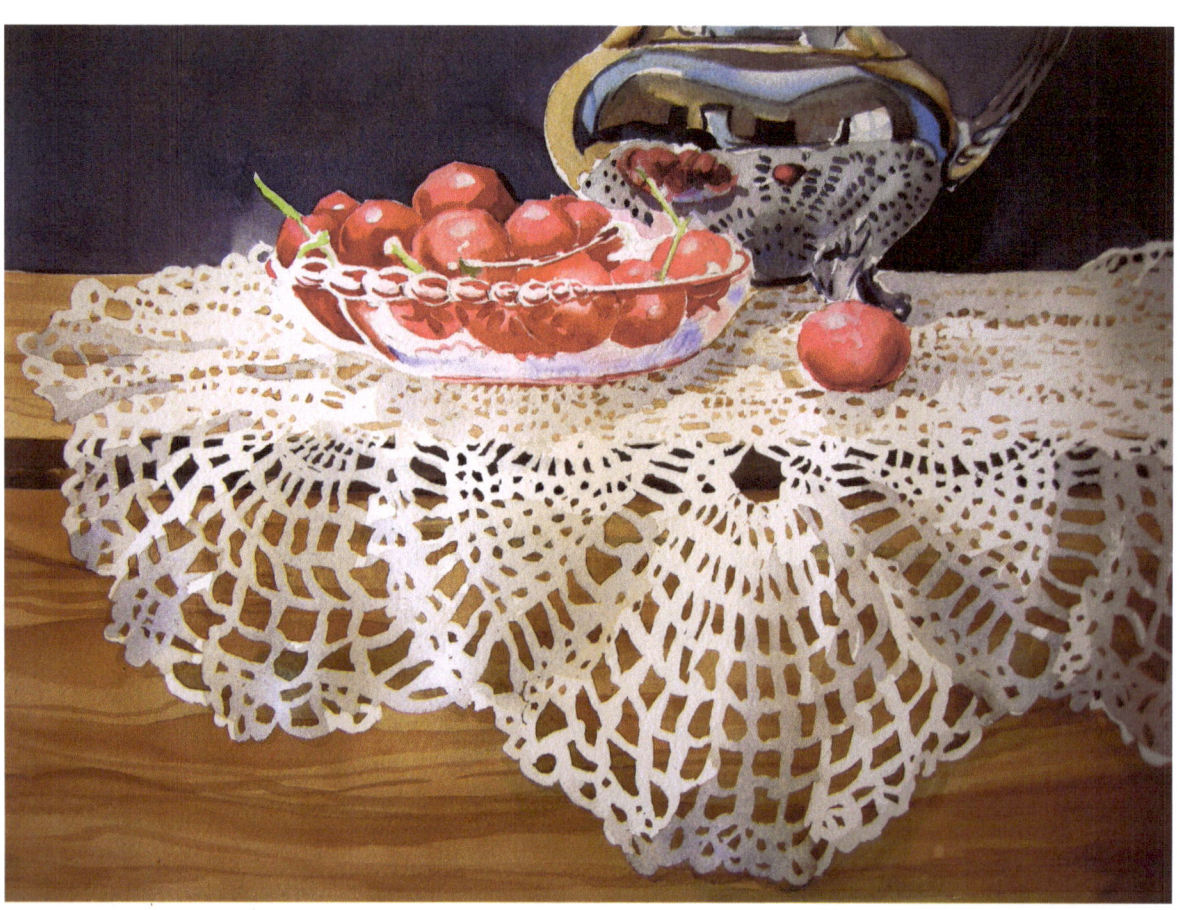

Final Details

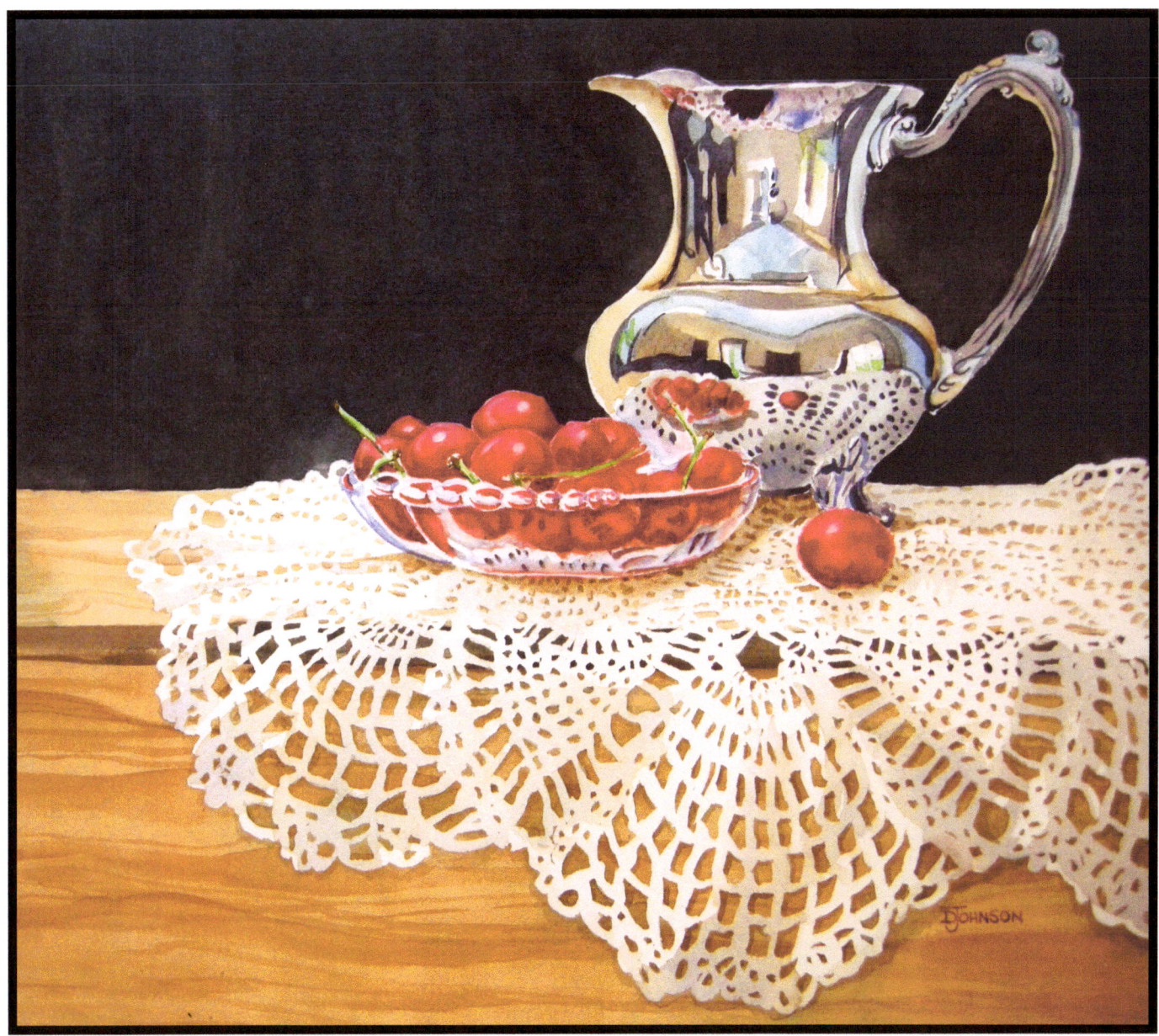

The final details are so important. I once heard someone say that if you think you are almost finished, stop!

Take a close look at my finished painting. I softened some of the highlights on the cherries with a moist brush. I glazed more reds on cherries, cool reds (Permanent Alizarin Crimson) in the shadows and warm reds (Winsor Red) in the cast shadows and midtone areas. I added another glaze to the background and inside the handle to darken these areas and make them more uniform. I think this added some drama.

I worked a little more on the shadow areas at the bottom and edges of the glass dish, and added some reds to the shadow areas under the dish and the single cherry. Finally, I added a glaze of Burnt Umber at base of dish and under pitcher to enhance warm shadows.

Reference Photos

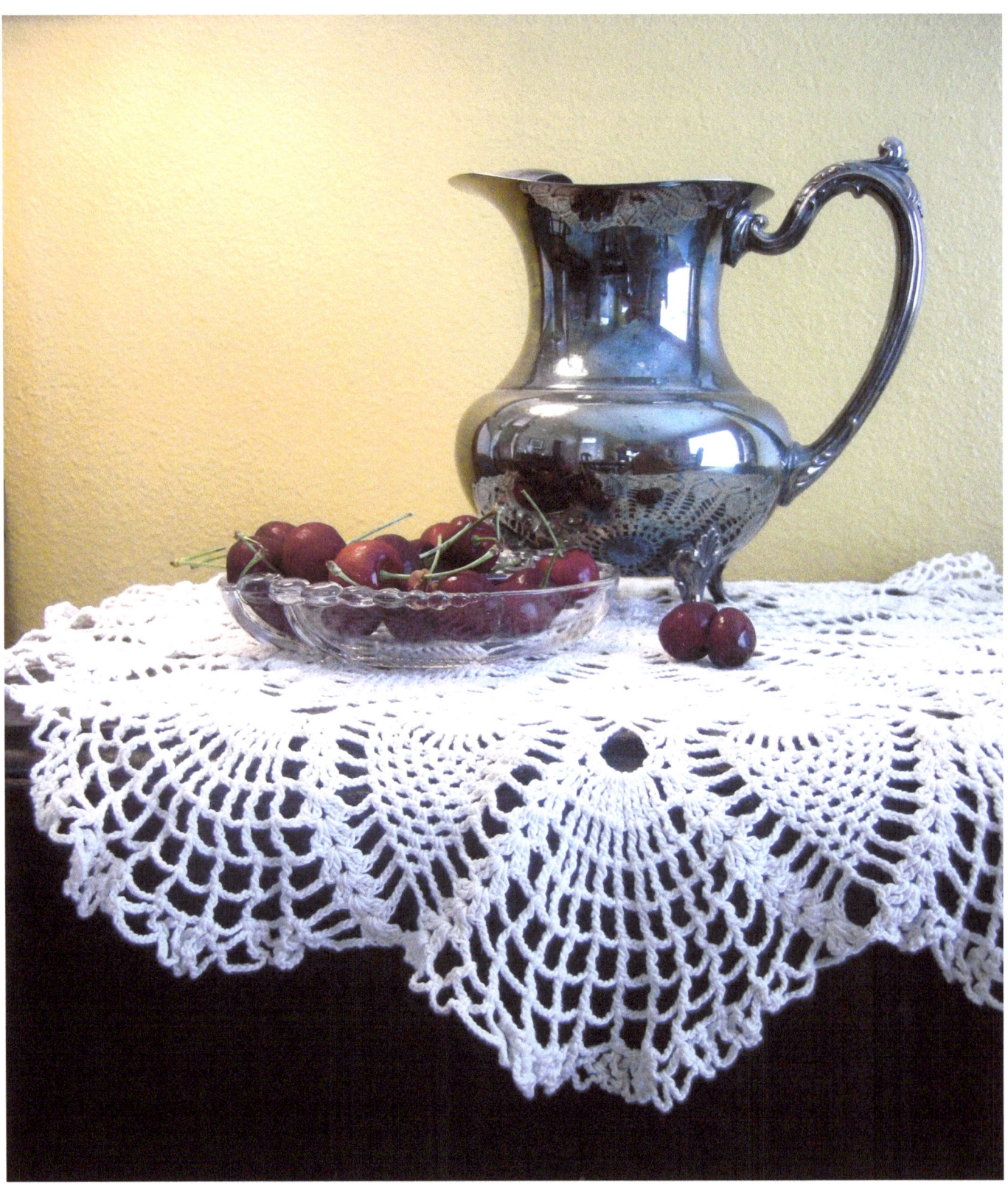

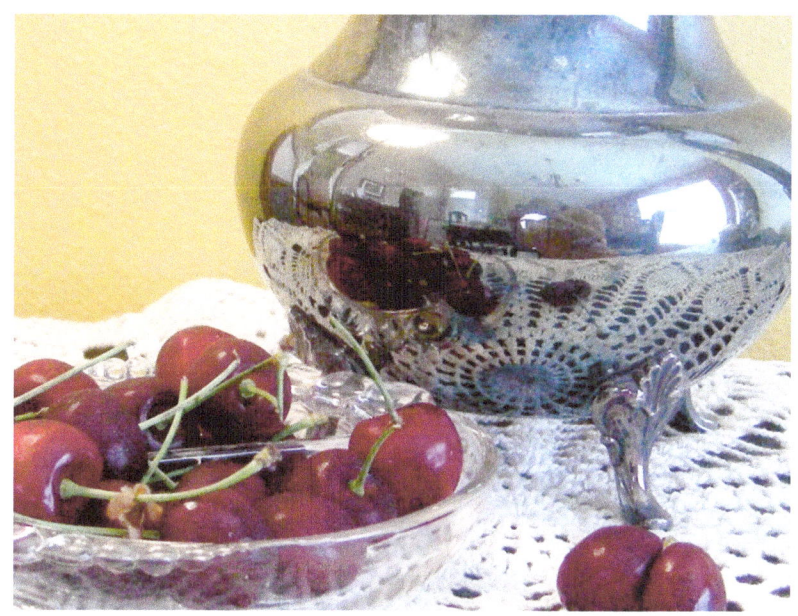

Detail view of cherries reflected in the silver.

Removing the color from the reference photo helps me to see the values – the lights and darks – that give the two dimensional surface of the photo an illusion of space and shape.

Look at the value chart below and try to see where those values are represented in the grayscale photo reference.

I hope you enjoyed this project. Please visit my website/blog and let me know your thoughts for future lessons!

www.debbiejohnsonartist.wordpress.com

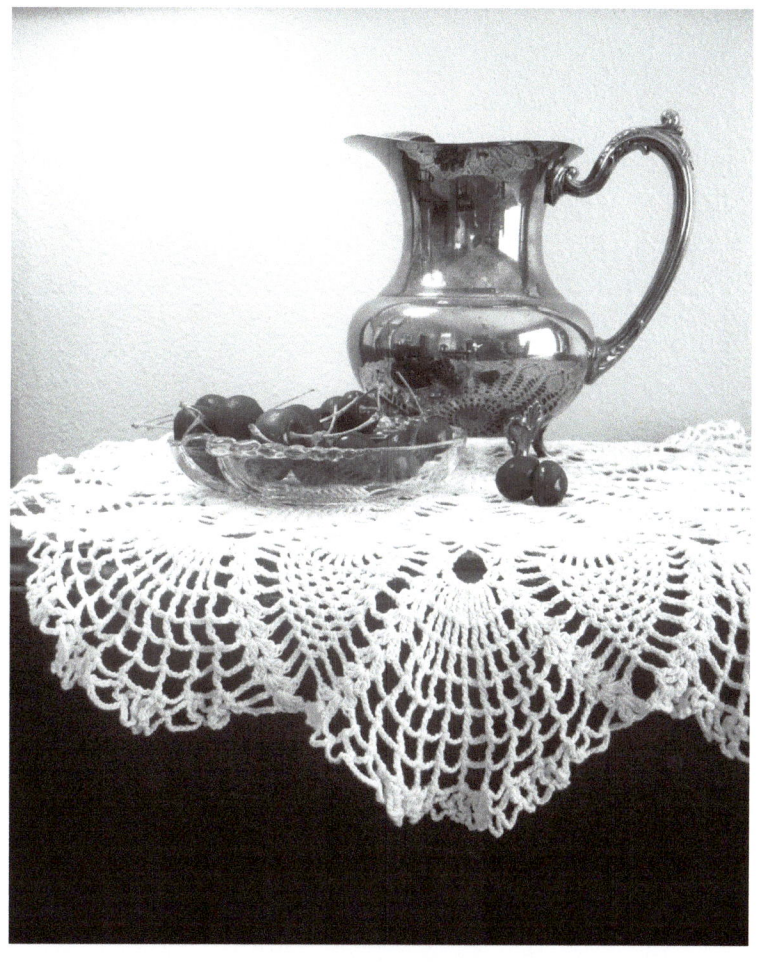

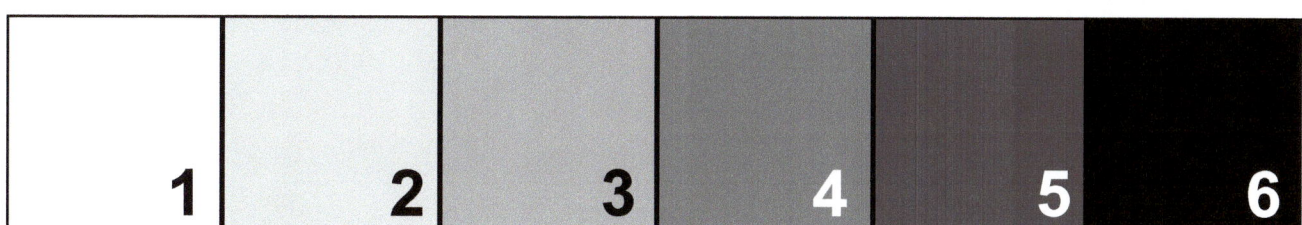

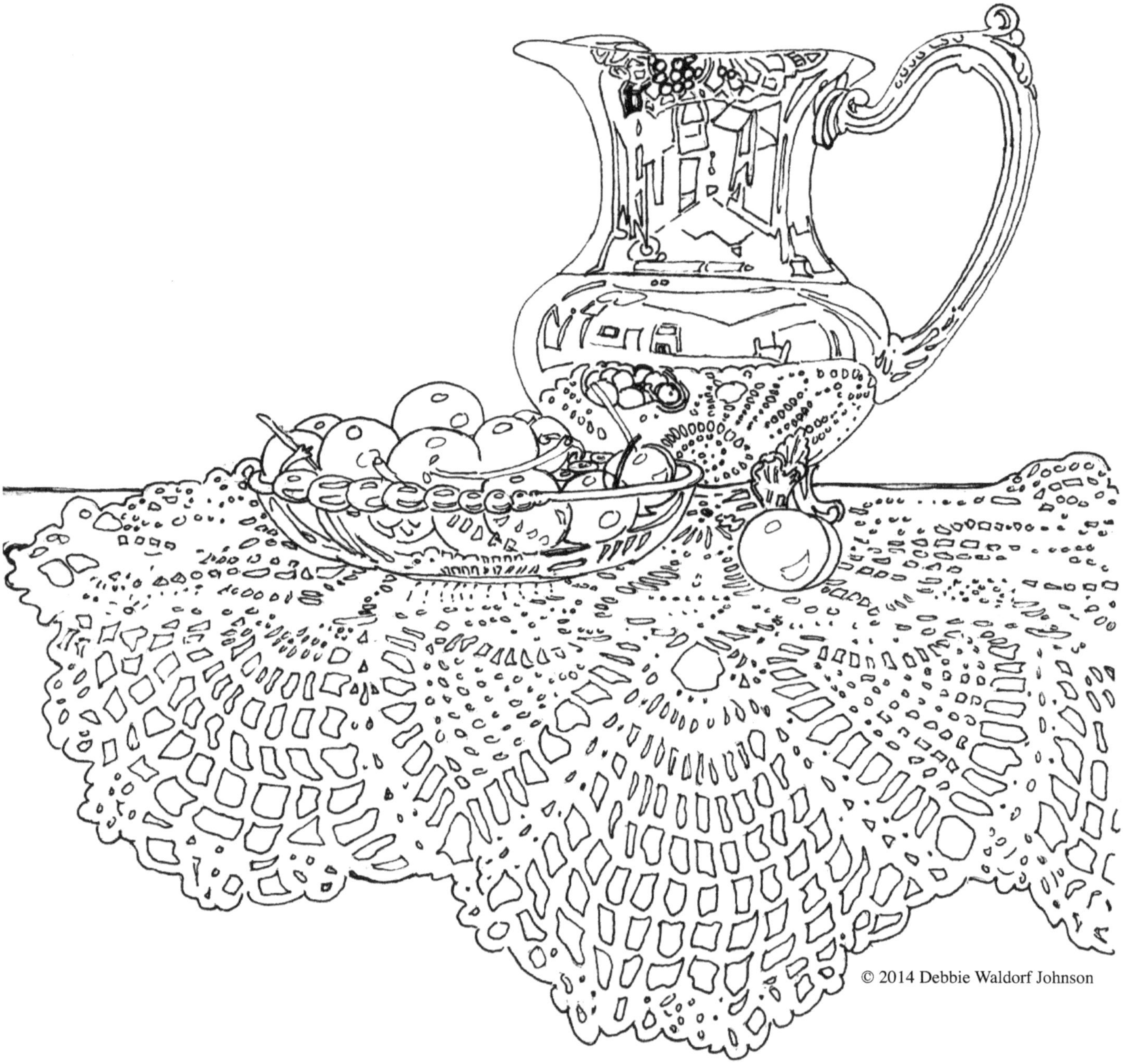

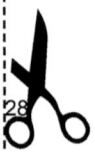

© 2014 Debbie Waldorf Johnson

This drawing can be traced onto watercolor paper for practice.
This page may be copied or enlarged for your personal use only.

Suggested Watercolor Supplies

- 11" x 14" inch pad of Arches 140 lb. watercolor paper, or larger
- One-inch flat brush, natural hair, or natural hair/synthetic blend
- Number10 round brush, natural hair or natural hair/synthetic blend
- Number 6 round brush, natural hair or natural hair/synthetic blend
- Palette with large mixing wells and one-inch or wider paint wells. My favorite palette is CheapJoes Piggy Back.
- Winsor & Newton (professional grade/not student grade) pigments: Aureolin Yellow, New Gamboge, Winsor Red, Permanent Alizarin Crimson, Burnt Sienna, Perylene Maroon, VanDyke Brown, Raw Umber, Hookers Green, Cerulean Blue, French Ultramarine Blue, Indigo. Any other colors you may like to use. Other good brands are: Maimeriblu, Holbein, and Daler-Rowney. Look for transparent colors.
- White vinyl eraser
- Sketchbook, any kind
- Large water container (1 lb. deli tub works great)
- Paper towels
- Number 2 pencil
- Two-inch wide masking tape (not blue painter's tape)
- Masking fluid
- Masking fluid brush
- Masking fluid pickup tool
- Two small containers for masking and soap

Have fun experimenting with colors, brushes, and techniques. Every artist has his or her favorite tools and methods which is what makes each artist unique.

Great Online Art Supply Resources:
www.cheapjoes.com
jerrysartarama.com
www.dickblick.com
www.aswexpress.com
www.utrechtart.com
www.artsuppliesonline.com
Be sure to check with your local art supply store first.

Debbie Waldorf Johnson has more lessons on her website:
http://debbiejohnsonartist.wordpress.com/Lessons
You will find step-by-step lessons in blog format as well as links to videos of how to correctly develop watercolor washes.

www.ingramcontent.com/pod-product-compliance
Lightning Source LLC
Chambersburg PA
CBHW050419180526
45159CB00005B/2339